HONEST RELIGION

By

JOHN OMAN

D.D., F.B.A.

With an Introduction by

FRANK H. BALLARD, M.A.

and a Memoir of the Author by

GEORGE ALEXANDER, M.A.

and

H. H. FARMER, D.D.

THE RELIGIOUS BOOK CLUB
121 CHARING CROSS ROAD
LONDON, W.C. 2
1941

First edition   Jan. 1941
Religious Book Club edition June 1941

CONTENTS

Honest Religion an aim not a possession. Questions of erudition to be faced, but answers not to be forthwith accepted.

Chapter I. THE SITUATION   1

Decay of belief in liberty and progress, with final problem God. Immediate cause the War, but only accelerated what is always. Disturbances both of faith and morals. Yet not worse than the Early Church. Danger of half-truths.

Chapter II. BACKWARDS OR FORWARDS   11

What is true lesson of our losses? Withdrawal or more instant use; returning to old authorities or more earnest search for truth? Custom and acceptance. Security in compulsion? What is God's order? Honesty and the highest. Denying the world to possessing it.

Chapter III. ARGUMENT   21

"Crisis" present watchword. Decisions not discussions. But faith wisdom for thought as well as action. Yet argument more for clearing ground than planting. Effect in science mechanism, in philosophy process, in theology infallibilities. Different kinds of greatness.

Negative honesty. Positive concerned with intuition and aspiration. Honesty about religion and honesty within it. God's permission to abuse His gifts. Power to do so from religion. Watershed in thinking. Is dealing with God for final or infinite ends? Three finalities—final organisation, final ideals and final theologies. Mystery. Paul's and Calvin's idea.

Honesty not limited by rules. Pioneers. Meeting failures. Spiritual succour and demand. No spiritual good merely given and God neither fiat nor process. Our part primarily temper—and right temper from honesty in life not from argument. Purpose of parables to present religion in life. Parable of the spade—cheerful adaptable industry, but without hardness or evasion. Misuse of higher world. Victory of Cross over both. Religion's sphere beyond seen, but not by ignoring the seen.

Via Media. Geniality and severity. A Gospel or an Ethic? Honesty to have grace or grace to have honesty? God's giving and our receiving not opposites, nor His revealing and our perceiving. Even Hebrew Prophets through material to spiritual: and by persuasion. Bible really history of reconciliation. Essential message and essential truth in Hosea. Value for it of stern experience.

Higher criticism may concern lower honesty, but lowest most testing. Accepted whole or rejected whole, both alike from idea that in revelation God's work is not man's nor man's God's. To be inspired to be helped to think—not submission to possession. Paul and the Law. Some conclusions of criticism. One failure. Mythology. From law to liberty; later from liberty to law. How Jesus built on Old Testament and above it.

Jesus and cosmology. Doctrine of Father greatest truth about world or greatest delusion. Rubrics of theology separate God and the world and man. Their relation the question. Yet real world what it is to serve and real man what he is meant to be? Revelation of Father in Jesus. Concerned with both. Faith in Father. Our Lord's view (1) of Nature, (2) of Human Nature, (3) of Providence, (4) of Prayer, (5) of the Kingdom of God, (6) of Immortality, (7) of Pardon and Grace.

Loss of infallible Church and Scripture. Temporal loss eternal gain? Different ideas of faith, freedom and tradition. Freedom needs honesty without fears, hesitations, compromises. Only from faith resting on God's good-news. In no worse position than Early Church. The past ours in freedom. Specially concerns Jesus Christ as ground of faith not burden on it. Nor by experiences but as all experience is interpreted by mind of God. Historical questions.

God the absolute power. Grace God's way of power. How Jesus has all power. Not in being omnipotent. Vastness and religion. Abstract substance, and the revelation of God's mind in all. Reconciliation to it in all. Titles in New Testament (1) The Christ, (2) The Lord, (3) The Son.

What of other things in Scripture? Revelation as imposed information and injunction. Paul's freedom. When we win it more agreement. John's Logos. Humanity means limitations. Jesus and the Kingdom. In what sense apocalyptic?

in all, but ever reaching beyond all. Turning necessity into freedom, and evanescent to eternal. Apostolic benediction. Mere vagueness? But through life and life as it is. Not ecclesiastical. God beyond knowing yet found by all who seek Him in the common ways. Saints. No models, but in way of purpose and succour.

Chapter XVI. WISDOM AND UNDERSTANDING

Prophet's tests. Problems of thought and action. Historical questions and dogmatic. Understanding to serve and test insight not over-rule it. -Ologies. Doctrine and ethics. Moral theology. Counsel of God.

Chapter XVII. THE CATHOLIC FAITH AND THE CONFESSIONS

Dogmas as creeds. Denominational and divisive. Polytheism and One Substance. Confessions—external heredity. Four purposes—apologetic, didactic, polemical, eirenical. Literal imposition. Covenants and election. Form and essence. Grace power, not power grace.

Chapter XVIII. THE CHURCH AND THE CHURCHES

Inward liberty and outward action. Heavenly vision—how obeyed? Authority within or without? State—ideal of Church. True unity. Fellowship and outward forms. Means or ends. No Church only Churches. Differences, even divisions not alienations. From our infirmities: perhaps needed by them. First unity then union. The Sacraments.

Chapter XIX. OUTWARD FREEDOM

Kingdom of God final order of all, not a special institution. Includes State. But State's method compulsion. Modification of method and limitation of sphere. Repudiation. Room for freedom, Church and State. The family. Divine. Freedom not from, but in, ties and obligations.

INTRODUCTION

BY FRANK H. BALLARD, M.A.

It was not Dr Oman's habit to be over careful for the future, but there was one thing impressed upon the minds of the members of his family, that no papers of his were to be published after his death. This book is, however, an obvious exception to the general ban. On the day he so suddenly and unexpectedly put down his pen and drew his last breath the manuscript was found on his desk actually packed and addressed to the Press. There were reasons, into which I need not now enter, why the work was not immediately published. Nothing has been lost by delay, for while there is much in the book that is pertinent to our present troubles, like all that my father-in-law wrote, it deals with abiding realities and will have its place whatever the shape of things to come may be.

Dr Oman more than once remarked to me that in a sense he had worked backwards. He began, in *Vision and Authority*, with an enquiry into the foundations on which all Churches rest. He was concerned with the Church, its authority, its creed and its organisation. He passed to what he believed to be the ultimate problem of the last two centuries, the relation of *Faith and Freedom*, "the problem of how Faith is to be absolute and Freedom absolute, yet both one". He returned to the first question in *The Church and the Divine Order*, confessing, however, that he was attempting no mere essay in ecclesiastical polity but a contribution to the problem whether our society is to rest on individual competition or legal socialism. In *Grace and Personality*, which is perhaps his profoundest and most original book, he developed ideas already stated in *Vision and Authority* and came to grips with ultimate theological problems. This was a war book in the sense that it was written when the nations were locked in mortal combat. Oman was by no means remote from the conflict. He was much amongst the troops, especially amongst the wounded, always ready to talk about the things that were troubling men's minds. There is, however, little of the shadow of war upon the pages in which we see "religion shining in its own light". The book was written in the conviction that "greater than all political securities for peace would be a Christian valuation of men and means, souls and things". At length came *The Natural and the Supernatural*, which some have regarded as his *magnum opus*, and which will probably rank as one of the greatest contributions to constructive apologetics this age has produced.

In none of these learned works was Oman out of touch with actual life. But he left much to be inferred —more than most of us could manage. Now and again—in, for example, *The War and its Issues*, *The Paradox of the World*, and *Concerning the Ministry*—he dealt with the practical difficulties of a work-a-day world, but he still left the impression that the whole body of teaching needed the kind of application he could do supremely well. This book goes far to make that application. It may not be as profound as *Grace and Personality* or as academic as *The Natural and the Supernatural*, but it is full of ripe wisdom and mature religious faith. All Oman's distinctive teaching is here, but perhaps more than in any other publication (with the single exception of the book on the Christian ministry) the man himself appears with his large knowledge of life and his sympathy with the troubles of the human heart.

Oman was scrupulously careful in the preparation of his books. He hated shoddy work and did his best to make each page accurate. We have tried, as time and ability have permitted, to respect his standards. Here and there we pondered sentences he might have rewritten, but beyond obvious verbal alterations making for clearness we have left the original untouched. Our work was greatly lightened by the very careful way in which the Press revision had been done. A word ought to be said about Scriptural quotations. The renderings do not always conform to any translation known to us, but so often the essential meaning of the passage is made clear and arresting that we decided to leave them unchanged. An interesting instance is the use of the expressive word "cheeped" in the rendering of Isaiah x. 14 on page 60.

The book, which is largely based on various addresses given in Cambridge, was read in MS by two of Dr Oman's oldest friends, the Rev. B. R. Mein and Mr George Alexander, and the latter has given me every assistance in putting it through the press. Oman and Alexander were fellow-students in Edinburgh and the friendship then formed never waned. Never, I imagine, was a major decision made in the life of either without the knowledge of the other. Readers of Oman's books will know how often he was indebted to his friend for help in reading manuscripts and proofs. They will be glad to read the brief memoir Mr Alexander has been persuaded to write for this volume.

It would not have been my father-in-law's wish that much should be said about him, but it was felt that something ought to be written about his contribution to theology and his place in the life of Cambridge. This has been contributed by his old student and successor at Westminster College, Dr H. H. Farmer.

The Index has been prepared by another old student, who became a son-in-law, the Rev. Frank McConnell, M.A., of Newcastle-upon-Tyne.

MEMOIR OF THE AUTHOR

I

BY GEORGE ALEXANDER, M.A.

Dr Oman, when discussing "Awareness and Apprehension" in his great work, *The Natural and the Supernatural*, describes how, as a small boy, standing by himself at the edge of the open sea, after being at church and hearing the difference between good and evil expressed "under the material forms of heaven and hell", the idea first came to him that he was alone, resulting in "a consciousness of myself which set me thinking, yet not about myself".[1] The whole passage is interesting, but enough has been quoted to show at how early an age Oman's environment stirred his reflective mind, destined as it developed to mark him out as "a man by himself", and foreshadowed a career which no one who knew him in his twenties could have forecast, least of all anyone familiar with the religious and ecclesiastical atmosphere of England and Scotland, even fifty years ago. No one else can well appreciate how, among many unexpected turns in Oman's career, the most unlikely was that the dreamy, shy youth who addressed fellow-students of his own Church with such diffidence, and at whom we were apt to smile, until we found he was always worth listening to, should have come to speak with confidence and authority to

[1] P. 136f.

men of all Churches, less in Scotland than in England, where lines are more sharply drawn, and have found himself so much at home in Cambridge with its academic life contrasting so strongly with that in which he was trained.

I may have run ahead, but it seemed worth while noting at the outset what, to all who knew him, was the outstanding feature of a career, in the critical years of which great thinking strove with limitations of oral expression, in circumstances where the value of the latter could not be despised and, so far as his chosen profession was concerned, narrowly escaped defeat.

John Wood Oman was born in July 1860, the second son of a family of four sons and two daughters, of whom since his death only one daughter survives. He was born in Orkney on the farm of Biggins, in the parish of Stenness (of Standing Stones fame) which ancestors had owned for hundreds of years, of which he himself was owner in turn and which is now in the possession of his eldest daughter, Mrs Ballard. His father, like so many Orcadians, had gone to sea in his youth and sailed for many years as captain, latterly of the mail steamer to Orkney. To his memory, Oman dedicated the Kerr Lectures, *The Problem of Faith and Freedom*, describing him as "a Scholar only of Life and Action, but my best Teacher". Did space permit, one might enlarge on what for an enquiring mind, to which, as Dr F. R. Tennant in the appreciative notice he contributed to the *Proceedings of the British Academy* remarked "a problem was a provocation", is the abundance of interest to be found within the narrow limits of the island home. Suffice it to say that, though he had not left home for his earlier education, the main part of which he owed to a tutor engaged for a neighbouring family and shared by a few other boys, it was possibly another proof of his individuality that he entered Edinburgh University at the age of seventeen with a well-stored mind, with anything but an insular intellectual outlook and more important still, with his native gift of original thought unimpaired.

Brought up in the United Presbyterian Church (now part of the Church of Scotland but in those days an active and uncompromising opponent of the latter as then constituted) Oman had decided to enter its ministry. The training involved an Arts' Course of normally four years, followed by three years in the Church's Theological College. It was the day of a uniform course for the M.A. degree without any of the options now permitted, to relieve the student of subjects less congenial to him and allow a certain amount of specialism. The examinations were taken in three departments—Classical, Mathematical and Philosophical. The last included papers in Logic and Metaphysics, Moral Philosophy and English Literature. Having taken a distinguished place in the classes (numbering from 150 to 200 students) required for the ordinary degree, Oman attended the advanced classes and graduated in 1882 with first class Honours in Philosophy. He also gained the Gray and Rhind Scholarships which were open to graduates of the University. The next three years were spent in taking the full theological course of his Church's College and, as the classes were recognized by the University for the degree of B.D. he added that to the Arts degree and a few years later the newly instituted D.Phil.

How the connexion began I do not know, but at that time students of the United Presbyterian College who wished to attend a German University for a summer term mostly found their way to Erlangen, and in the summer of 1883 Oman was one of three friends there, the others being Mr James Gardner, of whose early death he always spoke with deep feeling, and Mr B. R. Mein, ever one of his closest friends. He attended the lectures of Frank, Zahn and Class and perhaps owed his interest in Church Architecture to Hauck. The Theological "Verein" welcomed the Scottish students to guest membership and contributed not a little to the educational value of the term. Heidelberg claimed him for the summer of 1885 and there the chief attractions in the theological curriculum appear to have been Hausrath (New Testament Introduction) and Merx (Psalms) and he added lectures by Bartsch on German literature and Kuno Fischer on Faust. In his new surroundings his humour had full play and, from letters to his home, he enjoyed the summer. In August he went on to Neuchâtel, recommended to him for its climate and "being on a lake". There he spent nearly three months and gained a facility in French which, with his German, stood him in good stead when in later years he addressed Continental Churches.

After his return from Neuchâtel he was licensed by his Presbytery and put himself on the List of Probationers of the United Presbyterian Church with a view to obtaining a charge. That Church had its own method of filling vacancies so far as Probationers were concerned. A small Committee allocated vacancies among the Probationers who had no choice in the matter. After that, an appointment lay between the man himself and the congregation to which he, with the others assigned to it, had preached on two Sundays. The system was ideal in theory but, depending too much on pulpit gifts, failed, as Dr James Brown in the *Life of a Scottish Probationer* stated, to give "the same opportunity for men of high culture, who lack to some extent the power of effective utterance, attaining a position where their gifts can be used for the good of the Church".[1] The words were written years before Oman went to be assistant to Dr Brown, but he was already experiencing their truth. For a few months he took charge of a "preaching station" at Makerstoun, a few miles from Kelso, where he renewed association with a former minister of his in Stromness, Mr Kirkwood. As, however, he had to live in Kelso, and, as a rule, walk to and from Makerstoun for his services, he was not sorry to accept the Assistantship in St James's Church, Paisley, of which Dr Brown, to whom I have already referred, was minister. He was one of the leading men in the Church, a man of great charm, and he had a large and attached congregation. In Oman he found a man after his own heart and Oman always looked back happily on his time in Paisley.

During these months he preached in a number of vacant churches in Scotland, but his lack of what is known as a "good delivery" did not make up for the oft recognized quality of his sermons. Was it perhaps another evidence of his unusual personality that an older friend, himself a popular preacher, remarked that

[1] Pp. 82 ff. give an excellent description of the system and incidentally of a Probationer's experiences in Orkney.

he had never known anyone make such a clean division in congregations as Oman? The members were decided in their preference or their opposition, none seemed merely indifferent. The feeling of his friends that any congregation which did call him and have time to know him better would soon appreciate his worth was justified when towards the end of 1889 he was settled in Alnwick as colleague and successor to Mr Limont, who had been minister of the Clayport Church of the Presbyterian Church of England for many years, succeeding Dr John Ker, in his day a well-known preacher in Scotland and one who for pathos is singled out by Oman as one of six preachers he commended to his students.[1]

Dr Brown, though far from well, insisted on going to Alnwick to introduce Oman, to whom it was a lasting regret that a cold caught, on that visit, accentuated the illness which some months later carried off one of his best friends of an older generation. As may be supposed, Oman found himself in very different surroundings from those in which he had expected to serve, but he was already of ripe experience and his natural interest in all sorts and conditions of men made his new life easy to him.

It was a special pleasure to him that one of the members of the Northumberland Presbytery assembled to ordain him was Mr B. R. Mein (then settled in Thropton), who had accompanied him to Erlangen. It helped him greatly to have his old friend so near and to have his guidance while yet a stranger to the Presbytery, to both its members and its ways of work-

[1] *Concerning the Ministry*, p. 142.

ing. Though no ecclesiastic, it was not in him to take vows lightly and one soon heard of the place he was taking in the work of the Presbytery, and his desire to support weaker charges.

But his congregation was his first care, and if it was not long before he began his literary work, that brought no neglect of his people and there is evidence that they came to be proud of the wider notice he was gaining. He must have had their leave to give three courses of lectures, one at, I think, Auburn University, in the United States, followed by the offer of a Chair, one the Kerr Lectures, that appointment formerly in the hands of his old Church, the United Presbyterian, being then in the gift of the United Free Church, and the third being at Westminster College itself.

To Alnwick days also, Oman owed his first acquaintance with Miss Blair, daughter of Mr Hunter Blair, J.P. of Gosforth, which led to his marriage in 1897. Oman used to tell against himself that he took as the opening of the first service on returning from the honeymoon, the 67th Psalm beginning, "Lord bless and pity us". Pity, however, was the last term to apply to their union and Mrs Oman was able in the succeeding years in Alnwick not only to prove her capacity in the home and in the church work but to be the mentor which the rather absent-minded ways of her husband at times needed.

As the years passed four daughters were born and to those who saw him with his children in their earliest years, the stress he lays on the child mind in his writings is perhaps unconscious autobiography. He moved from Alnwick in 1907 to Cambridge on his appointment as Professor of Theology in Westminster College, and his congregation left Mrs Oman and himself in no doubt that the ties forged between members and minister would, as he hoped, be enduring.

The main part of the Cambridge life, I leave gladly to Professor Farmer, one of several former students Oman lived to see occupying Chairs. There are, however, one or two points of a more personal nature which may be worth recording without disloyalty to the memory of a friend to whom I have owed so much.

Oman had adapted himself in Alnwick to a Church life very different from that which he would have found in a Scottish town of the same size. He now, as I have already said, faced in the residential system of Cambridge an academic life, poles apart from that of Edinburgh in his day. The University admitted him, as other Westminster Professors not already Cambridge graduates, to its privileges by conferring the honorary degree of M.A., and he became a member of Queens' College and later on an honorary Fellow of Jesus. It was not long before he was on friendly relations not only with theological scholars of all Churches and views but with men eminent in other fields of knowledge. Of the many amenities, however, of the new position, he valued none more than the closer relationship between Professor and student, possible in a residential College. To be with him on a Sunday and find his students dropping in for tea or a smoke was to realize a relationship a classroom by itself could never give. And it was here, if I may say so, that Mrs Oman came into her kingdom. Her interest in the men was natural and unaffected. They could talk to her freely and her memory was of the order to call forth some kindly recollection of a student years after, if his name cropped up. To her Oman dedicated his volume of sermons, *The Paradox of the World*, and than ΣΟί, ΓΝΗΣίΑ ΣΎΖΥΓΕ no three words he ever penned, albeit a quotation, conveyed a greater wealth of meaning or more of himself.

The war of 1914–1918 brought an interruption of the College life but none to Oman's activities. The months spent in Birmingham with a small number of students, maintaining the services of vacant churches, visitation of military hospitals and the spell of work in France for the Y.M.C.A. still left time for expanding an address on the war he had given at Queens' and publishing it as *The War and its Issues*—a book, had he lived, he might well have re-issued in the light of this war.

He paid two visits to Germany after the last war During the occupation of the Rhineland, one of the Societies for improving international relations asked him to accompany two Swedish representatives to visit the prisons in which Germans were confined, and make a report which, I think, was private. It happened to be the time of inflation and his humour found outlet in the millions of marks he paid for a meal while his sympathy went out to the distress of the poorer people. The second visit was at the end of 1935 when he gave a paper to a meeting of the Student Christian Movement in Berlin. The paper was read for him by Mr Mackie, but he answered questions and took part in the discussions for two hours in German. Amongst others he met Niemöller, and on his return, at the request of

Dr John Hutton, he contributed his impressions to the *British Weekly*.

In 1931 he was called by his Church to the Moderatorship of its General Assembly and gave a notable address on Creeds with special reference to the Westminster Confession. During his Principalship both Oxford University and his own University, Edinburgh, conferred on him the honorary degree of D.D.

He had succeeded Dr Skinner as Principal of Westminster College in 1922, and when he himself retired in 1935 Mrs Oman and he at first thought of making a new home elsewhere, but after looking round for a year Cambridge drew them back. There was no sign of impending tragedy and every prospect of a pleasant retirement among old friends. No sooner, however, had Mrs Oman put the new house in order than she was struck down by what proved to be a fatal illness and she passed away just before Christmas, 1936. Oman never really recovered from the blow. A weariness crept into his life, though he was always ready to speak of his good fortune in the loyalty and devotion of his daughters and his younger sister, who had now made her home with him. He found distraction in work, including work on this book. But when in July 1938 he was offered the Fellowship of the British Academy, though he appreciated the honour he hesitated at first to accept, as he felt no longer able to do anything more "to support the honour". In 1938 also, by appointment of the British Academy, one of his oldest friends, Professor A. C. Welch of Edinburgh, gave the Schweich Lectures on Biblical Archaeology. Only reasons of health prevented Oman from being present.

For some time it had been known that he was suffering from weakness of the heart and a more serious attack had confined him to bed in May 1939. He was not thought to be in any immediate danger but he passed away with startling suddenness on the 18th. When a few days later he was laid to rest, the assemblage in the Presbyterian Church of Cambridge was a remarkable tribute to the position Oman had gained and to the wide range of scholarship and interests with which he had been associated.

There was in Oman's life much of the unexpected but no one can deny that "the deep things of God" were his first interest and that he had the highest ideal of his calling. Had he permitted, much could be added of his influence not only on students but among brother ministers. It cannot be said that he never had to face opposition and somehow he often gave a false impression of himself. But beneath the dreamy appearance there was a practical mind as well as a knowledge of human nature ready with sympathy or rebuke as occasion required. His friendship once given was never withdrawn: differences there might be, but at the worst there could be agreement to differ. In nothing did his foresight prove more accurate than his attitude to the war now upon us. We may be glad that he was spared what the Church of England Prayer Book, never with more aptness, calls "the miseries of this sinful world". He described in his book on the last war what he regarded as an ideal peace: may we hope that when the new peace comes it may be as Christian as the ideals for which we fight.

II

BY REV. PROFESSOR H. H. FARMER, D.D.

Looking back now on Oman's work in Cambridge as theologian, teacher, and trainer of men for the Christian ministry, it is possible to discern more clearly something which was increasingly felt as the years of his life passed. This was the unity and consistency which pervaded all that he was and said and did, a unity and consistency the more remarkable and impressive because of the unusual power and range of his mind and its interests. There was a massive integrity in Oman which comprehended within itself as much the small change of his everyday personal contacts as his deepest researches as a theologian and philosopher. This always in the end made itself felt for any who had more than a merely superficial contact with him, and was undoubtedly one source of his deep influence on his students, even on those, of whom there were usually some, who found his teaching and writing difficult, even at times incomprehensible. The meaning might baffle them, but there was no mistaking the unitary weight and stature of the man behind and within the teaching and all his personal dealings with them.

The secret of this massive unity is at once easy and difficult to state. Underlying his integrity in the sense of "wholeness" there was a remarkable integrity in the sense of "sincerity". Yet, and here is the difficulty, "sincerity" in its ordinary usage is a poor, thin word to indicate what is meant. To quote some words I have used elsewhere, "in Oman sincerity was a broad, steady, powerful, open-eyed, confident, mature— every adjective is necessary—intention to grasp and be grasped by the truth over the whole range of experience and knowledge, no matter how it presents itself". That truth is not truth for you until you see it for yourself, that it will assuredly be given you if, and only if, you seek it with all your powers—these basic themes of his teaching found impressive embodiment in himself. There was none of his students who did not feel somewhat daunted by his superlative equipment of knowledge and insight, but there was none also who did not feel the inspiring rebuke which daily met them in one who so plainly scorned, not in word merely, but in his whole person, the "unlit lamp and ungirt loin". Some were wont to think of him as a somewhat formidable person; others wondered sometimes whether he understood the difficulties of the not too bright student; others, again, thought him somewhat intolerant of views with which he did not agree. No doubt he had the defect of his quality. But the quality was such that when once it was felt the defect counted for little. Indeed in this instance the defect was perhaps not altogether a disadvantage. It was good, perhaps, that Oman's challenge to sincerity was such that one could always, if one were foolish enough, take shelter under a complaining desire for more tender treatment.

Yet Oman's austerity had a deep, if reserved, sympathy at its heart, as many of his students have learnt from experience, and the only thing he really required of the not too bright student was that he should use such powers as he had to their fullest pitch.

The intolerance, moreover, which he seemed to display towards views with which he disagreed was certainly sometimes due, not to the fact that he disagreed, but to the fact that he sensed in them an underlying insincerity, a thinking *à parti pris* which to him was not thinking at all. Nor was he any other than a humble man. There is no sincerity without humility, as there is no humility without reverence and faith. It was because Oman's sincerity was integrally bound up with his reverence for God, and his understanding of His purpose in the world, that he was able to send forth many students deeply changed by their sojourn at Westminster College. He gave to many of them a new vision of God, of life's true meaning and use, of the ministerial calling, which has stood the test even of these grim times. His continuous insistence, for example, on the difference between mere solemnity in religion and worship and true reverence, or again, on the difference between a preacher who respects his hearers because he reveres God's purpose with them as persons and a preacher who merely seeks to manipulate them by popular artifice, was not only salutary for his students, but was in fact a clue to his whole religious and theological outlook.

Here again the unity of his mind and character discloses itself. For Oman's theology might well be described as the theology of "reverence, freedom, and sincerity". We could indeed describe it as the theology of God's personal dealings with men, but that would convey little. All Christian theologies must maintain, at least verbally, that God values and deals with men as persons. What distinguishes Oman is the profound consistency with which this is wrought out into every department of religious experience and theological reflexion under the guidance of the three categories already referred to—reverence, freedom, and sincerity. In what is perhaps his greatest work, *The Natural and the Supernatural*, man's capacity to apprehend the sacred and to respond (or not to respond) to it in reverent obedience is made the clue to the nature and history of religion, and through this to the understanding of human personality, of evolution, of history, of man's place in and apprehension of the natural order, the whole constituting a mighty argument to justify the contention that to know the reality of the supernatural environment, the prime requisite, as in other spheres, is to be willing to respond to it and to live in its midst with sincerity of mind. In *Grace and Personality* the same basic position is worked out in relation to the doctrine of grace and reconciliation with a thoroughness, originality and spiritual power which makes the book, to use Dr Tennant's words concerning it, "one of the major treasures of theological literature". In his other books the same basic theme is applied to other central issues: in *Vision and Authority*, to the problem of authority; in *The Church and the Divine Order*, to the doctrine of the Church; in *The Problem of Faith and Freedom in the Last Two Centuries*, to a critical review of movements of thought from Pascal to Ritschl.

Oman's magnitude as a profound scholar and original thinker was, it is hardly necessary to say, fully recognized in the University of Cambridge. He was thrice appointed to the Stanton Lectureship in the Philosophy of Religion and for many years served on the Board of the Faculty of Divinity and on its Degree Committee. He was frequently called on to advise university students reading the philosophy of religion, and through these activities, as through his lectures and books, he came to be one of the main influences in the study of the philosophy of religion in Cambridge. The following has been written by one of the Professors in the University:

On the Faculty Board, though not himself directly concerned with the details of University routine and administration, Oman's learning and wide range of scholarship, and his deep interest in education as something much greater than mere instruction, gave great weight to his opinion on all questions that concerned the policy of the Faculty. His service to the Degree Committee was especially notable, and it was far from being confined to opinions on works in the Philosophy of Religion. His shrewdness and humour, and his dislike of sham or pretentious work could make him a severe critic where severity was deserved; but his judgment was always generous in its recognition of good work and of promise, especially in the young student. His knowledge of men and things, his great powers of observation, and that direct and profound acquaintance with simple and unsophisticated things, which was one of his outstanding characteristics, gave sureness and originality to all his judgments, and enabled him always to penetrate to the heart of the matter. Members of the Faculty who learned from his wisdom and enjoyed his friendship cherish their memory of him as among the most original minds that have contributed to theological studies in recent times.

The same writer, referring to a remarkable autobiographical passage in Oman's review of the English translation of Otto's *The Idea of the Holy* in the *Journal of Theological Studies* (it is unfortunately too long to quote; the review, along with other reviews he contributed to the journal, should certainly not be missed by a student of Oman), writes in a letter:

The paragraph impressed me in 1924 as it does still. There is his insight and power of criticism, his humour, his wonderful observation, and the glimpse of his boyhood in Orkney which must, I have always supposed, have meant very much to him in his later work and thought. When I think of the great man, heather, and salt winds, and mountain mists come to mind rather than a gown and lecturer's desk; and his thought is the profounder for this. There is an interesting parallel here in James Ward. They were very different men; but both were great figures in philosophy in Cambridge; both knew many books, and knew them better for knowing other things as well; and each owed much to a boyhood spent amid natural country.

Of Oman's place in the history of theological thought it is obviously too early to speak. Yet there can hardly be any question along what lines his main contribution has been, and will still continue to be. It is hinted at in the title of this, his last book, which thus rounds off and completes the unity of his mind and work: *Honest Religion*. It is the holding together in close-knit and indissoluble unity with one another on the one hand the self-authenticating nature of God's disclosure of Himself to the human spirit, so that it requires neither the proofs of philosophers nor the patronage of secular moralists to establish its right to our utmost allegiance, and on the other hand the inviolable dignity of the human person as one called in freedom to know the truth, if he will, over the whole breadth of experience. There is always a tendency for these two things to fall apart, as is evidenced by some contemporary theologies. A religious experience which claims to stand in its own right and to shine in its own light is always in danger of becoming divorced from rational reflexion, from ethical responsibility, and from the concerns of daily life. It is, in fact, in danger of becoming a refuge from reality, of becoming *dishonest* in the deep and challenging sense in which Oman used that term. If the deepest need of these days is for the recovery in our midst of religious faith which has the springs of power within itself, is not apart from the stuff of the common life, secures, amidst all the forces tending to destroy it, the significance and worth of the human person, and, finally, can claim the allegiance of men's most mature, strenuous, and sincere thought, then Oman's theology is wholly to the point and must remain so for many years to come. Certainly no competent theologian will be able to ignore *The Natural and the Supernatural* or *Grace and Personality* and no theological student ought to be allowed to.

AUTHOR'S PREFACE

Seeing how many have found justification for intolerance and persecution in the assurance that honest conviction is their peculiar possession, it may be necessary to explain that the title *Honest Religion* sets forth an aspiration after what has no limit or finality, of which the essence is humility towards God and charity towards man, an ideal for all but not an attainment by any, and certainly not by the author. Rather it speaks of what, had I been patient enough I might have found, wise enough I might have valued, humble enough I might have possessed, kind enough I might have used to higher service.

But while this may be left to appear in what follows, there are many affirmations, especially of a critical nature, which, as they are obviously contrary to much erudite opinion, may well be regarded as in need of further defence. Unfortunately this could not be done within reasonable limits, so the conclusions will just have to go for what they seem to be worth.

Yet I should like to say a word in justification for taking them on their own merits without much deference to learned support or assured result of criticism.

The central question concerns the Gospels and in particular the views of the various German Schools regarding them. That researches have had great value for raising the essential questions, knowledge of which is a necessary equipment for the study I do not question. But I am far from being as persuaded of the value of their answers.

Through four of these movements I have lived. This, in itself, may be some justification for not surrendering one's liberty to any of them. Each alike appeared in its time as an oracle, with disciples multiplying the echoes till it was taken to be the one emancipating truth, with all other opinions as mere prejudices of the unenlightened. Possibly it may be mere contrariness, but this business of oracles and schools seems another reason for defending one's liberty. All alike drilled life and history into accord with some intellectual abstraction used as a battle-cry, and saw only with the spectacles of the particular theory. This also seems another challenge to one's liberty, and while an abstract theory might be useful as a hypothesis for research, as a universal principle it cannot but be an imposition on the fullness of life and history.

The Tübingen School, when first I became interested in the subject, though past its glory, had still to be treated with respectful argument. It did a great deal to foster the useful idea that history shows the fixed and accepted as still fluid and in conflict. But its method was to drill facts into accord with the Hegelian categories. Moreover, its claim that these embody the absolute philosophy which orders Christianity into an absolute religion, gave it the privilege of claiming to be the only royal intellectual academy. No subsequent school has risen to quite this height of glorifying the abstraction as universal oracle but they have all followed in some way and in some degree.

From the Tübingen School the Ritschlian was a revolt, but though partly saved by Ritschl's discovery of the individuality of Mark's Gospel, it was in the main

determined by another abstraction. The supreme error
of the Tübingen School was taken to be its pantheistic,
non-moral interpretation of Christianity. Against this
was set up, as the central concern, the Kingdom of God,
interpreted as the progressive moralisation of the race.
But the Kantian type of ethics tended to become just
another category, and entirely failed to show why the
mould of moral form—the Pharisee—did not go into
this kingdom before the publican and the sinner. The
School was less Olympian, and their contribution to
raising the essential questions about early Christianity
much greater, yet their answers were determined by
their outlook, far more than their outlook by their
answers.

The Apocalyptic School was a revolt from the
Ritschlian, having the special mission to deny all that
was rational in its predecessor's view. But by the
spectacles of its theory its vision was even more controlled. Nor was its theory so radically different as is
assumed, because it still continued to measure with the
old Kantian ethic, if not the old Kantian reason.

In *Mein Leben und Denken* (p. 50) Schweitzer says that
"Jesus accepts as true the late Jewish Messianic expectation in all its externality. In no way does He attempt to
spiritualise it. But He fills it with His powerful ethical
spirit." If, however, there is anything certain about
what Jesus did, it was to work a moral regeneration by
a religious one, and that His ethical spirit was not of
the Kantian order to be merely poured into anything.
Surely Otto's statement is beyond question that there
are "two different expectations in Scripture, one,
the establishment in glory of the people of God—a

thoroughly political idea—and the other the religious
and moral revival of their deeper life and enhancement
and unfolding of their faith, with extension to the
heathen: and that Jesus deliberately chose the latter, the
very acceptance of His messiahship meaning the renunciation of the dreams and hopes of the former, the result
being a new piety, a liberating, redeeming childlike
trust in the Father, which lifted its possessor above all
servitude into eternal love" (*The Life and Ministry of
Jesus according to the Historical and Critical Method*, p. 39).
But Schweitzer manages to ignore all this by going
through the whole history of Synoptic Criticism and
having no regard for anything except what he calls
"consistent Apocalyptic". Surely the application of
such conformity, and calling it consistency, to such a
person as Jesus in an age of such cross-currents as His, is
self-condemned. To me, at least, nothing seems clearer
than that the whole Jewish expectation was transformed
by a quite different spiritual outlook, and that, only
after the Fall of Jerusalem, and, from Jewish sources, a
more material apocalyptic took possession of a section
of the Christian Church. How, for example, if the
burden of the teaching of Jesus had been such apocalyptic, does Revelation, one-third of which at least is
quotation from the prophets so interpreted, not have a
single quotation from Jesus Himself?

The most recent School tests all by "form" and what
it calls "seat in life". This might seem to show more
regard to life and history, but, in point of fact, it is used
just as another category to drill the records and has a
great part of its impressiveness from becoming the
slogan or battle-cry of a school. Yet this which has given

it vogue, seems to me its main error. Every idea it uses has been said casually and within limits before; and there is nothing it says but may in certain cases be true: only it is not so universally true that a general ordering of all can be derived from it.

This differs, however, from the previous movements in being a continuation of its predecessor not, as always before, a revolt from it.

Its fundamental postulate is thus stated, "A community of unlettered people, who to-day or to-morrow expected the end of the world, had for the production of books neither capacity nor interest, and we may not ascribe to the Christian Community of the first two or three decades any really literary activity" (Dibelius, *Formgeschichte*, p. 9).

But, in the first place, how do we know that the early Christians were all unlettered? Paul certainly was not, and the people who could read and understand his letters with sufficient interest to preserve them, might well have been able to record at a very early date the sayings and doings of Jesus and to have had interest in doing so. Amos sprang just from such people, and he was a great writer. In the second place, how do we know that they lived in such immediate and constant expectation of the end of the world, that we may not attribute any literary activity to them? Amos was a good deal of an Apocalyptist, the writers of the Enoch literature were more, and the author of Revelation wrote an elaborate book though he thought the end came quickly. If for thirty or forty years or so much was remembered about Jesus why should there not have been interest to write it down, especially as it was obviously preserved by quite

other interests than expectation of the end of the world?
Moreover, it is plain that this interest alone did not
preserve the Pauline literature, and its existence proves
at least that the Early Church knew the value of writing.

Nor is what is said of the form more convincing.
That the form of the narratives was produced by a law
of popular preaching is pure assertion. Except two
examples from Luke, all are in Mark, and the style of
Luke's narratives is not in the least similar to Mark's.
Jesus was a preacher who set an example of condensed
picturesque narrative, and the tradition that Peter, who
learned of Him, recorded these stories in preaching and
that Mark repeated from him, goes much better with the
individuality of the style, which is not in the least like
any popular preaching known in this country or any
other, least of all in Germany. What is done by repetition
in preaching appears in Matthew, where the interest in
the narrative is subordinated to the homily, with matter
brought together for no other reason than edification,
and the lessons expanded from the Old Testament.
There might be no conscious literary standard or desire
for literary distinction. But has that ever made for
true literature? Moreover, we quite underestimate the
accuracy with which teaching, regarded as sacred,
would be remembered by people not dependent on
note taking. For example, I am not in the least sure that
Matthew and Luke had a common written record of the
teaching of Jesus, nor am I sure that even when using
Mark it is not from memory.

On the other hand, however, were we sure that we
had a narrative written within six weeks of the event,
we could not be certain of the absence of all exaltation

of the marvellous, because this takes place while the wonder is still active and the narrative fluid, not afterwards when it has become cold and stereotyped. The result is that we can be far surer of the teaching than of the narrative, for if the latter present a true enough general picture, it is only so on the whole, while the former is, almost without question, the most exact reproduction of speech in all human history.

On the purport of this teaching I find myself largely in agreement with Professor Otto's view that Jesus announced a Kingdom already present in spiritual power but which was to have further manifestation and consummation, yet this was to be of the nature of the prophetic vision of knowing God and having His commandment in the heart.

My difference from him is in his view of the Holy. To it he ascribes the power of Jesus; and to prove his case he gives examples of the awe Jesus inspired. But in the Gospels they are obviously related as exceptions, under the stress of circumstances, to His general bearing.

Professor Otto was interested in the Holy just as intense emotion, and I do not question its power in certain conditions and for certain ends.

One evening I walked down to a public meeting with General Booth. He was talking like a common mortal on common things, when suddenly he was surrounded by a band of the faithful, and, in a moment, his speech, his bearing, even his appearance, were transfigured, by what was an afflatus and not an affectation: and I realised that, given a slightly different age, there would have been nothing his followers might not have believed about him. In the meeting, however, what it did was to give intensity to the accepted, not only in idea, but in phraseology, and was quite obviously unfitted for any purpose of new insight or even new presentation. But could anything have been more different from what the Holy meant with Jesus?

It is like the difference between experienced sensation, by which the sensational school sought to explain all perception, and its actual place in the process, wherein its significance is in quality not intensity and it so rapidly passes into action and by it to objective reality and we only dimly know the road we have travelled by tracing it backwards. The higher reality, without which no perception is human is, I have contended, similarly known, only the feeling is the sense of the holy and the action on the absolute obligation of the sacred. In Jesus we see that this sense is the varied responsive reverence out of which love has cast all fear and the obligation the perfect loyalty out of which joy and freedom have cast all servitude. Wherefore, our honesty comes so much in the end to be concerned with the faith of Christ, and seeing The Father in His face, because we arrive only as our reverence is love and our service liberty.

J. O.

1939

CHAPTER I

THE SITUATION

STRICTLY SPEAKING no book was ever written except in the first person, and it is not modesty to say, "This is merely my opinion on my limited experience", for no human verdict on anything is ever more. Whether this remain mere personal idiosyncrasy or objective truth is not by any separation of reality from our knowing, but depends on the justification we have for thinking that our subjective assurance is due to our laying ourselves open, with utter honesty, to its testimony. In every sphere the failure is less in discovering little, than in not finding the attitude of mind and interest and service which could have discovered more.

Search for Truth and Righteousness is just accepting God's invitation to "Come and let us reason together"; and my general purpose is to ask what a true response would mean, or in other words, what bearing and attitude would be entire honesty in making life a continual reasoning with God in the sense of laying our minds alongside of His and open to His persuasion.

But as God has admitted all kinds of queer arguments from men and led them on by them, so it is fitting for us to exercise a large charity about what may have been a help at one time even if it became a hindrance to progress at another, even to the absence of such charity itself.

"In proportion", says Gardiner, "as the student of the history of the seventeenth century perceives clearly that religious toleration was the goal to which it was tending, and that in it alone could its difficulties find its appropriate solution, he is tempted to think hardly and bitterly of those men who turned their backs upon such a benefit. Eliot and Winthrop would hear as little of it as Laud and Wentworth." But the student of history, he thinks, should draw wiser conclusions and entertain more charitable feelings, for an advanced opinion is like an advanced invention, requiring a corresponding progress in other things to make it possible or desirable.

In the days when Gardiner wrote there seemed good reason to believe that the time had come when this freedom was possible and would be a benefit without drawbacks. The old insistence on one Church with one creed and one constitution had only resulted in many sects, and liberty had diminished their virulence without apparently weakening their loyalties. The age was full of cheerful discussion and agreeable social intercourse. If some were disturbed by ideas about a mechanical universe, they were sustained by the assurance of a continuous upward thrust of progress. The churches were full of people who were honest, kindly and liberal. There might be the muttering of criticism about the Bible, but it was mainly over the Old Testament and did not seem to threaten any vital part. Life probably never was so secure in all the ages or material well-being so abundant and easy for so many, and if to some it seemed to go on so well of itself that God was a superfluity, to the great bulk of decent people it meant the additional assurance of a wise and good Providence, the due and becoming recognition of which was public worship, practical liberalities and an upright walk and conversation. Beyond this was the sense of blessings above desert, though the blessings themselves rather conveyed the sense of merit; and there was much confessing of sin, though it was apt to be conventional, like "your humble servant" at the end of a letter.

The blight to fair expectations, the uncertainty of life, the burden of the years were as in every other age, but progress in every field of knowledge hid the abysmal depth of human ignorance about what it most concerns us to know, and invention and enterprise helped to forgetfulness of man's impotence to supply his deepest needs and secure his highest well-being. Wherefore, the time seemed favoured above all the ages; and, to the reasonably successful, their place in it highly satisfactory, so far as this expressed itself in religion, it was by faith in a genial Christ, who offered guidance, help and good fellowship and other aids to playing one's part well, and who called men to amend society, unite the Church and convert the heathen.

If the Church itself was called in question, what it stood for seemed secure; if the Bible was less of an authority, much of what it taught was preached by every great writer. Nor is it doubtful that even a vague faith and rather formal relation to the Church did much to make decent hard-working citizens with kindly relations at home and abroad and some serious respect to duty and regard for society and the right direction of the State. With all its faults, it was no mere age of machinery, great as were the changes wrought thereby, but it was a time of widespread kindly humanities and of extended enlightenment, as well as of great minds and great thoughts, in which it was good to have lived.

But to-day we are asking whether the belief in liberty and progress, which was its chief inspiration, is sustained either by religion or reality. Were men not so comfortable with freedom, because they had not really thrown off the old authorities, but only made them sit more lightly while still holding the reins pretty firmly? Now, however, that their enfeebled hands no longer control, whither are we tending if not to the abyss? And as for the assurance of even progress, did it not rest upon a quasi-scientific belief of a necessary progress overruling all deficiencies of our purpose, which was neither freedom nor religion?

If religion can still work by freedom, at best it is a slow business of the ages, the more doubtful now that the comfortable doctrine of Providence, on which the hope of its attainment rested, seems to have been blotted out in the blood of the young and their mothers' tears. It may have flourished in the summer sunshine, but what is its value if it is like the sap of the dahlia, which dries up at the first touch of frost, and is not, like the maturing of the rose, a preparation for enduring the winter?

The immediate cause of the War may have been the machinations of wicked men, and their guilt is not condoned because God might have overruled it. Yet the final problem is just God, because, for what He could have hindered and did not, He, or at least the purpose He has to serve in allowing its course to human responsibility, must be the justification, if there be any; for in the end, we have to say with the prophet: "Is there evil in the city and the Lord has not done it?" The destruction of possessions may be profitable, the more perhaps if painfully acquired, and necessary if not profitably used; and no one has ever had any lease of life. But what mockery that the supreme triumph of the science in which youth trusted, was to blot out millions of their lives and shatter many more, and leave still more broken-hearted and desolate. With the Psalmist our real trouble is not calamity, but the fear that the sufferings of the innocent may show the government of the world to be indifferent or blind or unjust. Above all, what kind of consistency can this have with the Father of Jesus Christ?

When, however, we look facts in the face, we realise that the War has done nothing but knock the spectacles of familiarity and custom off our eyes.

1. Nature unceasingly works the same destruction of human lives and of all man's handiwork, slower it may be, but more thoroughly and on a still vaster scale. In the days of comfort and cheerful human intercourse, of high hopes and youthful vigour, we could easily overlook what the Apostle calls "the bondage of corruption". But the real grip of this slavery upon us has never relaxed. Death and decay were always busy, and the bright hours were always swifter than a weaver's shuttle, man went to his long home and the mourners went about the streets, and dust and ashes was the end of all our human achievements.

2. God always gave scope to human sin and folly. What a man sowed he reaped, and God did not intervene to prevent the calamitous harvest of a sowing of wild oats. Vice ruined constitutions, wrecked homes and digged untimely graves. Pride went before falls, often dishonourable falls, like dishonesty, the criminal

court or suicide. Even thoughtlessness had consequences of appalling severity.

3. There has always been solidarity in evil as well as in good. What Paul called the flesh we called heredity; what Augustine called original sin we spoke of as defective evolution. But under either description it meant that children suffered for the sins of parents, and subjects for rulers, and that every tie that knits men together can be turned to community in evil as well as in good, to building up a kingdom of darkness as well as of light.

Nevertheless nothing is the same for us mortals when the emphasis is either increased or changed. The most important difference is the fear that liberty may not be able to meet the increasing distress. Of its failure in the State we hear on every side, but, as freedom is a religion or it is nothing, the essential failure may be the Church. Why has the Church, in all its organised forms and activities, fallen into such weakness? Is it not the undermining of its compulsory, legal, externally authoritative basis? The denial of toleration might not have saved the situation, but is not the result of toleration just what those who dreaded it feared? Revelation is no longer submissively received as Divine legislation, attendance at worship is no more meritorious; directly or indirectly the Church no longer controls faith or morals. There are empty churches and full cinemas, and questionings of the fundamentals in conduct as well as creed, with no doubtful effect in unsettled lives and disturbed family loyalties, and preference for anything rather than serious responsibilities. Finally, with the loss of the legal view of redemption as an external transaction, the churches themselves have been left with no very obvious gospel, resulting in a tendency to allow sentiment to do duty for thinking, impression for persuasion, repetition of ancient formulas for living convictions and of antique resonant language for simple and sincere devotion. That they have lost influence with workers who are the real body of the people and who, as they handle life with ungloved hand, should naturally be the most religious, may be a calamitous loss for the serious ordering of all human relations, but we are the further from repairing it if the churches are not appealing by what ought to be heard, received and served.

Nor is anything else doing much to replace the loss. If life provides a whirl of variety for some, it demands a monotony of drudgery from others; and the lack of times of reflexion is not well replaced by increased distractions. Life in consequence has not grown deeper as it has grown wider. Even education has done little to redress the balance. Few prophecies have been less fulfilled than the high hopes of the Victorians from universal education. It has exposed many minds to greater ephemeral distraction, but how much has it done to increase discernment of the eternal amid the fleeting, of the elemental amid the trivial, or for that matter of independence of judgment of any kind? Even in more advanced instruction, the abler have been put into blinkers and driven in the ruts of specialism, while the less fortunately endowed wander aimlessly, loaded up with promiscuous encyclopaedic information. Neither way has proved much help for looking round one's whole position with wisdom and a responsive mind. Had the churches, when they were in power, not far greater

claim to have made people of character and wisdom?
And were not good Evangelicals and High-Churchmen
justified in all their fears of Liberalism of every kind?

And does not this Liberalism spring from one root?

Doctrines are of three levels. Religious belief is an
emotion stirred by an idea, and the first level is just for
common expression of a general experience, such as
reconciliation to the Father by the manifestation of His
love. This speaks only to those who have the experience.
But emotions have to be conveyed indirectly by calling
up common thoughts which may be translated back
into a common experience. This produces the second
level. Thus the Apostle presented his good-news in a
way which he could sum up as the grace of our Lord
Jesus Christ, the love of God and the fellowship of the
Spirit. This was a compendium of the Gospel he had to
preach, but one he meant to be known by being re-
experienced, and it assumes the fellowship of those it
would influence and who have at least the beginnings
of a response. As all the members of the Early Church
were in this position there was no need of any other
form. But soon many came in attracted only by the
more decent behaviour and higher tone of the Christians; and then, after Christianity became the religion
of the Empire, there were even less Christian forms of
attraction. This produced a third level of dogmas as
authoritative mysteries on the authority of the Church
and the Bible, which was sufficient when the Church
ceased to be a family and became a State, because so
general an institution as a State must be satisfied if its
laws are not actively opposed or its organisation openly
departed from.

The conception of the Church, as Bellarmin puts it, which is as much a State as the Kingdom of France or the Republic of Venice, took final form when the Empire fell and the Church had to do its best to introduce order into the chaos. And while the Reformation called this claim in question, it not only transferred the same authority to the Bible, but assumed that in spiritual things the authority of the Church was not greatly altered.

The crisis for this whole conception of religious authority was the age of Rationalism, not merely because, with the rise of historical criticism, both authorities lost much of their infallibility, but because of the denial on principle that this kind of external rule was consistent with the responsibility of a grown man for his beliefs and actions, and the affirmation that only what we see to be true is truth for us and only what we judge to be right is righteous.

This is the principle of freedom, and the chaos of our time would seem to be its outcome. But is the cause freedom itself or failure to rise to its responsibility? This is our supreme question.

Among the most disturbing forms of proving our freedom has been the habit of shouting half-truths as slogans. At one time immanence was invoked to explain everything, with man as the incarnate divine; at another the only truth was transcendence, with God on one side and human pride and slackness on the other. At one time the world order was a fixed rule with no place of repentance; at another every colour was needed for the picture. At one time it was man's infinite perfectibility; at another it was a contempt for man compared with which total depravity was adulation. At one time it was the thrust of the even upward progress of evolution, at another it was crisis with even progress a vain illusion.

If, however, slogans are produced by freedom, it is not in order to make us free, but to create a kind of general authority to relieve us from the burden of personal insight, inquiry and decision. This may provide shelter in schools as well as in churches: and the way they are accepted is the worst kind of surrender of freedom, all the more dangerous for our honesty that their fashions are always presented as the last word in mental and moral emancipation.

CHAPTER II

BACKWARDS OR FORWARDS

TO-DAY not only the earth but the heaven has been shaken; and both may have been needed, for the worst effect of thinking our outward lives secure was not material ease, but being at ease in Zion. The fashion of a time was too easily accepted as the pattern on the Mount; the routine of respectability as the high calling of God; and contentment due to indifference and unreflecting habit as God's peace. To save us from thus glorying in progress, measured by comforts and privileges, no disaster might be too great. And for the failure to follow insight and face calls the needed lesson may have been to allow man's own wilfulness to lead to its own disaster. Even war might be better than turning life into a perpetual blind alley, with the present in itself as the end and not as the way to better things.

Yet, what is the right lesson? Is it only to teach the evanescence of the troubled years of our mortal conflict? There have been times in the history of the world when this life with all its belongings seemed to shrink to nothingness. Usually they have been times of prolonged material disaster, when civil order was overturned and life insecure and one sowed what others reaped, as at the first great irruption of the German races over Europe. Then ancient civilisation became a remote memory, and religion was turned, with ever-increasing emphasis, into a business of another life and the preparation for it by a life of discipline and prayer, with nothing but heaven and hell of great importance or any certainty, while placidity in this life and security for another was found in an authority dictating faith and directing morals.

Honesty requires us to face the fact that the surest of all certainties about life is death. But is it to use life's uncertainty to evade its claims, or to be a constant spur to seize upon its fleeting opportunity? If life is short for possession, it can be very long for missing its calls and opportunities unless we are instant in season and out of season to make the most of them. Yet if all endeavour is vain not merely from the material world being shaken, but still more from the heart being distressed with doubts and perplexities and our footing being in shifting sand, have we not a right to weary of the long road of freedom and to seek peace in contemplation, under the shadow of an old and revered authority?

To many there seems at this time no other hope of peace, so they seek to persuade themselves that it is not the voice of God that has shaken the earth and the heavens, but is merely the failure of man's voice to maintain the old infallibilities, which, seeing that at the same time man is said to be naught and God all, is neither honest nor convincing.

This anxious looking back is further confirmed by reaction from the kind of re-building at present in vogue, which merely shows inability to learn any lesson. The bricks have fallen, but we will build again with hewn stones of possession as better tools for slaughter and of knowledge as greater power for destruction. The temptation is to meet this by building again the spiritual walls with hewn stones of greater domination,

which may offer the hope of keeping our faith apart
from the uncertainty, the evanescence, the unpredicta-
bility of events, the untrustworthiness of human associations, which more than ever we have seen to fail us
in the few and evil years of our mortal conflict. The time
may, therefore, be near when men may no longer wish
to relate their earthly problems and tasks to their
religion, but seek to use religion to escape from them.
And among the most distressing problems from which
to escape will be the long and dubious search for truth;
and among the most burdensome tasks, the humbling
and little successful endeavour after justice and social
righteousness.

Yet we may not blind ourselves to the dangers and
disasters of our unsettled state when no final standards
of belief or conduct are left, and negation is called
honesty, and self-control repression, and self-analysing
psychologies have no place for objective truth, and self-
absorption assumes our interest in seeing it naked in
autobiographies and novels, though more unpleasant
and less decent than the physical exposures treated as
criminal and regarded as indicating a feeble as well as
perverted mind. Should we not then, as Jeremiah in a
similar time, announce as the word of the Lord, "Stand
ye in the ways, and see, and ask for the old paths!" And
what are the old ways if not an infallible Church or an
infallible Bible or both, and the way to walk therein
submission to their authority!

Yet Jeremiah's call is not to walk in them. It is to
stand in them, and, by reflecting on them, to find the
right way and therein to walk. There is no breadth of
judgment without help from the past, but there is no

using the past to good purpose without independent judgment on it of our own conscience of truth and right. And if the old foundation was not so tested, may that not be the reason why the bricks are fallen; and may it not be as foolish in religion as in politics to say we will build thereon with hewn stone?

Moreover, in life it is very seldom that the way through is the way back. Freedom is leaving the flesh-pots of Egypt and facing the wilderness, and the reason why we are lost so long in the wilderness and make our way so slowly through it, is the old one of turning back in our hearts into Egypt.

Finally, can we honestly persuade ourselves that the old external authorities are among the things that cannot be shaken? For most people, though criticism may have shown the Bible to have more meaning, it has made impossible any honest return to the idea of it as infallible Divine legislation. A Catholicism which thinks that God kept the Church right for four or five centuries and then allowed the Papacy to run away with it, makes Him too like some generals who were good with a division, but helpless with an army. Nor is it easy to be convinced by the claims of a Papacy which rests on St Peter, whose strong point was never infallibility, claims, moreover, which seem to show God to have been as blind to the significance of a German monk as the Pope or the Emperor. Nor are those who know something of the spirit of toleration ever likely to admit that toleration was merely of man's slackness and not of God's mind; and the defence of the Inquisi-tion as an eminently just tribunal shocks them as a denial of what they are most assured is Christian.

Nevertheless, even among those who would agree with this, there is a hankering after seeing the Church become again an impressive institution, its doctrines having the prestige of dignity and antiquity and its Bible accepted as a solemn and impressive legislation.

As of old, this turning back in our hearts has been because freedom has not been a challenge to high enterprise, has not said, we are well able to go in and possess the land. Too much it has been a saying of "Peace, Peace, when there is no peace". The churches are troubled, but it is about their numbers, their finances, their enterprises, and not about what alone matters gravely, their message and the embodiment of it in their own fellowship.

Even such a matter as going to church as a custom is not unimportant. Were all virtue lost that depends on keeping good company, we should all probably be startled with our poverty. As the custom helped to encourage serious thought, sustain upright conduct and foster the spirit of consideration, its decay even as a custom is not replaced by anything else. Yet, when the individual has no root in himself, custom is an unreliable substitute and has always been apt to fail when most needed.

Wapping Quay, it used to be said, was the most religious spot in the British Empire, for there the Scotsman left his religion. But if he could leave it for so slight a reason as a change of surroundings, though it may be that for outward conduct and social decency the loss was great, religiously it could have been little. One of the most distressing experiences of the War was to see lads brought up like the young ruler, who, in the ordinary life with its safeguards, could have said even to old age, "all the commandments I have outwardly kept from my youth", whose religion and morality were in the army like tow in the flame. But, on the other hand, it was also plain that, by any serious religion, however unorthodox, unchurchy and perplexed, men were guarded, which only showed—what the prophets of all ages have declared—the worthlessness of merely formal religion and merely external influence. What, therefore, the War did, was not to take away what we truly possessed, but to show what we only supposed we had.

Freedom may have losses over which we grieve and responsibilities which are burdens we do not carry lightly and often not at all. A century of experience may, therefore, modify the exuberance with which men first hailed its birth as "Happy are all who have been permitted to breathe the morning air". More clearly than they did, we see that the Church is "shaking in its gross temporal pillars", but we may not be so sure that it is "strengthening its spiritual foundations". Yet the result shows that they needed strengthening. And that discovery itself may be the necessary beginning of better things. A faith which challenged neither thought nor action, and a loyalty which was partly custom, partly the accepted order, and partly a deference not quite free from superstition, had strange failures while it lasted and was always liable, when challenged by changes of thought and new conditions, to perish. And if its religion was only a trust in Providence which could be blotted out by the blood of the young and their mothers' tears, its loss when it was needed most only reveals its worthlessness.

As I have lived mostly among earnest young people, I am not without the assurance that, in spite of everything, even now our gains outweigh our losses. The mere freedom from the feeling that their religion is imposed upon them is itself a great gain. There is more courage to live their lives, and a freer comradeship between the sexes, and a concern for the poor and the weak, and a willingness to serve every higher cause. This leaven of earnest, thoughtful, reverent, patient, consecrated young lives may be small, but an influence which spreads through its vitality has more to do with quality than quantity. The dissipation of life in distractions and the valuing of everything as it provides them is vastly more obvious; but the obvious is seldom the most important and never the most enduring.

Yet how we measure security depends on whether we think a truth is held when none dare gainsay it or right right when none dare do otherwise, or that truth is truth for us only as we see it to be true, and right only as we judge it to be right. In short is either truth or right ever truly or rightly possessed except in freedom?

Here is where our difference becomes fundamental, in practice even more than in theory. Outward chaos distresses some, and for them the great matter seems to be to get the right beliefs accepted and the right service done, with emphasis on all the outward helps. To others the most distressing thing is lack of thought and low motive, and mere outward conformity to orthodox faith or accord with publicly approved action of little value without personal conviction and personal consecration.

If God is of the former persuasion, we cannot say that

His place in history is obvious. It is not only that the movement of recent centuries towards freedom of mind and conscience, as the responsibility of every grown-up person, seems to have been inevitable in its progress and to be undeniable in its result, but is there any sense in history or, for that matter, in life itself, if God's first concern is merely that His will be done, and not with how it is done? If it be all-important in God's sight that we should hold correct doctrines and belong to the approved institutions and accept in our actions the right official direction, surely He could have had no difficulty in securing this from the beginning. Why should He have confined infallibility to the Papacy, and even to it within such narrow limits, when He could so easily have made us all infallible in every belief and our actions as correctly ruled as a planet's?

If however the sole perfect order is knowing God's truth of our own insight and doing God's will of our own discernment and joyful consecration, and that what distinguishes children of God from mere works of God is just search for truth however imperfect and aspiration after righteousness however inadequate, we can have some understanding of the need for the painful and wandering way man has had to travel, with its errors and its sins, its divisions and its conflicts. Or, even if we do not understand, we can at least press forward in the assurance that, if it mean a world order in each person's insight and consecration, the road cannot be too long or hard to be worth while.

But it is worth all hazard only because to know of our own insight and serve of our own consecration is the final order, including our right relation to all other things, both the heritage of the past and the possibilities of the future, as well as all the requirements of the present. Therefore, the negative, intellectualist, self-sufficient, self-satisfied freedom of rationalism is only a kind of conceit of a youth who has wrung from a too authoritative parent the possession of a latchkey, without realising that, at the same time, he has taken over the grave responsibility of guiding his own life, in which he might well profit from his parents' experience. But, though the parent may see the folly of this and fear the pitfalls, he is a foolish parent if he still wishes to hold his son in tutelage. And this tutelage itself has been wrong if it has not been looking forward to the day when his son would undertake the responsibilities of manhood. Even the negative freedom of emancipation is not won rightly or safely except through the positive way of accepting responsibility. But responsibility is just life's greatest burden, and a large part of human history consists of the efforts to throw it off.

When honesty is reduced to its most negative idea of not believing anything not to be proved in a demonstration by logic, and not doing anything that is not required by the principles of reason, it can give a high sense of self-satisfaction in being enlightened by persons who obey the imperatives of conscience, and it may even find peace of mind in identifying the very idea of religion with dishonesty. But a true honesty is ever haunted by the fear of missing the highest and failing in the best, and it is guided by a humble search and patient aspiration which has little concern with mere argument.

Though I hope that what follows may be understood

of itself, I am in a sense travelling forwards on a road I have already travelled backwards, and shall therefore be compelled occasionally to assume what I have already done my best to justify. But most of it is in the last paragraph of *The Natural and the Supernatural*, which I may be allowed to quote as setting forth the position at which my former studies had arrived, as the starting point from which I now begin.

"If we have any content in the eternal it is from dealing whole-heartedly with the evanescent; if we would have any content in freedom it is by victory both without and within over the necessary; if we would have any content in mind and spirit we must know aright by valuing aright. If so, religion must be a large experience in which we grow in knowledge as we grow in humility and courage, in which we deal with life and not with abstractions, and with God as the environment in which we live and move and have our being and not as an ecclesiastical formula. This we realise, as all environment is only to be realised, by rightly living in it. It is for our knowing, but only as in the courage of humility we submit our minds to the witness of all that is to be known; it is for the victory of our freedom, but only as we accept the discipline of what cannot be altered and endure the burden of the duty of altering what should be changed; it is an eternal possession, but only as we grow in the eternal wisdom through life's changes and do not imagine that any other abiding possession can be in the evanescent. Denying the world does not mean that we do not possess it in courageous use of all its possibilities, but only that we do not allow it to possess us."

CHAPTER III

ARGUMENT

IN his *Journey to the Western Highlands* Dr Johnson tells of meeting an aged minister who had the most venerable appearance he ever saw and whose conversation was not unworthy of his appearance, yet some of whose good will he lost by treating a heretical writer with more regard than in the old man's opinion a heretic could deserve. "But", says Johnson, "I honoured his orthodoxy and did not much censure his asperity. A man who has settled his opinions does not love to have the tranquillity of his convictions disturbed; and at seventy-seven it is time to be in earnest."

Being in earnest obviously meant refusing to make religion the subject of a bout of argument: and this might be a good resolve at any age and about any matter of importance. Yet asperity would rather seem to show the sourness than the mellowness of long life, and trouble rather than tranquillity about convictions.

If it mean a closed mind, no age justifies it, but it is rather the danger of advancing years most to be resisted. Now that I have come to a like age, I would fain be able to agree with Friedrich von Hügel. From his brother's house, which was next door, he one morning walked into my study: and, as he entered, he said, "I heard you were here, and have come to make your acquaintance". Then he went straight on. "You know that my brother is an Orthodox Catholic, and he thinks me hopelessly juvenile: but, when I cease to take in new ideas, I hope they will order in the undertaker."

This was, however, in the last generation, and the present would doubtless find the hopelessness in a senility out of touch with our distressful time, and not in juvenility. Our serious-minded youth, in an age of which "crisis" is the chief watchword, feel justified in asperity towards all ideas that would hamper prompt, decisive and united action. And more particularly they think the very cause of the crisis and of wavering and weakness in dealing with it was the craze of their predecessors for what was worshipped as freedom of thought and action. Possibly, in the comfortable Victorian age, such luxuries could be afforded, especially as men were able, in spite of their differences, to act together on still uncontested moral standards. But, to-day, is not all this love of new ideas and freedom of conviction concerning them plainly seen to be mere detachment from the urgency of our time and subjective thinking in face of stern objective realities?

In one sense every age presents high decisions before God which makes it a time of crisis. But even were it so in the highest degree, is it the temper of faith to turn either man's rule or God's into a slogan, and to offer one device after another as the way of salvation, with much waste of breath on high sounding platitudes?

Is not the deepest conviction of faith just that God's rule is, in the end, the only environment, and man's rule enduring only as it is in accord with His? And, if so, can any disaster in human affairs, any disappointment of hopes and ambitions, any undermining of foundations or shattering of securities, or even any shaking of the deepest assurances of our spirit, be a crisis which should hinder us from possessing our souls in freedom and patience? Is it not the very business of religion to give us the calm wisdom which does not lift up its voice in the streets, but which allows us to reflect when we ought to reflect, as well as to act when we ought to act: and which finds both its strength and its guidance in waiting upon God?

Yet while waiting upon God is reasoning together with Him to clear our minds and understand His, it is neither arguing with Him nor about Him.

Argument is a good tool for plucking up or breaking down, but not for planting and building: and, though it may be needed to clear the ground before we can do either, in rough hands it can be destructive to what can be planted only by insight and built only by consecration. To mere argument the most obvious reason is the weightiest: and the obvious is often only what we are too short-sighted to see beyond. Thus it may become merely an easy way of stripping reality of its perplexity and so of obscuring its profundity.

Dr Johnson's old acquaintance may, therefore, have had better reason for resenting argument than a mind closed to new truth—the sound reason that long experience had taught him to distrust it as a means for reaching any truth worth knowing.

Of the effect of argument in blinding men to the wonders of the world of their commonest experience, with the most deplorable effect on the possibility of spiritual discernment, perhaps the greatest example in all history has been the confidence with which a Mechanical Physics was argued from, as not alone true but the whole truth. Though the wonders of the world were all about men, they accepted the desiccated picture of the universe as a not very intricate sort of mechanical toy, at the bidding of a theory which even Physics to-day shows to be inadequate for the marvel of a single atom. Nevertheless, dressed up in imposing technical phraseology, it occupied the seat of infallible authority, and regarded all other interests as merely obscurantist intrusions into the temple of truth, with thought and enquiry on higher values, especially religious, as forthwith a disqualification for the exercise of any honest judgment.

The Physicist, being forced, by first-hand dealing with the subject, to realise the limit of his knowledge and the uncertainty of his theories, especially disclaimed this new high-priesthood. The Biologist, having the assurance, which, in this perplexing world, is only given to second-hand knowledge, and being more distracted from interest in moral and spiritual values, not by science, which simplifies, but by having only facts towards science, which are ever increasing in number and complexity, was more ready, for a time, to accept the role of supreme pundit on all things, which third-hand knowledge, gathered mainly from popular encyclopaedias and shilling handbooks, was ever ready to impose upon him. This prestige was further strengthened as Aesculapius became the chief god of the Pantheon, with all his methods mainly determined by this kind of mechanical Biology. Thus the Biologist was able to overlook the plainest of all facts about life, that it works by preference as a motive before, and is not life at all if it be merely response to impact from behind.

But, for Biologists also, the times are changed. At least the more independent minds have already come to the conclusion that the great bulk of what professed to be science is only the building of one hypothesis upon another and that what is actually known by observed and proved evidence is very little. Further they are beginning to add that, even if we know everything about organisms, instead of our knowledge stopping just when it becomes interesting, Biology would still cover only a small part of life as a whole, and that the less important.

Moreover, as scientists multiply, they become better known as men of like passions with ourselves. "The learned after all", says one of them, "are men, and are readily impregnated by the prejudices of their environment and their time." They have even, he thinks, special temptations to limit their outlook by what may only prove to be temporary scientific pre-conceptions. "The very eminence of specialists makes them more dangerous, as those who are distinguished in a special manner by great discoveries or useful inventions come to believe that their knowledge of one subject extends to all. Edison, for example, does not hesitate to impart to the public his views on philosophy and religion."[1]

But Edison had also the support of being a successful man of business, which is not only a more effectual safeguard against the humbling and perplexing effect of higher interest, but confers assurance in delivering judgment on all things in heaven and earth, compared with which science is mere hesitation, the more so the more scientific it is. For this there are two reasons. Material

[1] Alexis Carrel, *L'Homme Inconnu*.

success is the most obvious commendation of our superiority; and honesty being a costly virtue, it is natural for the rich to think they can best afford it. To know facts and weigh opinions is regarded as essential to honesty in all other concerns; only in the highest, and particularly in religion, honesty is assumed to be purely a matter of argument without bias, except against what is of no consequence.

Like a good many more of my contemporaries I have spent much breath arguing against such argument. But now I see that its conclusions never had any support except the nature itself of argument from an abstraction, which is to detach itself from experience and work as a pure mental exercise in the void.

Perhaps it is myth that Galileo discovered the laws of motion by dropping stones from the leaning tower of Pisa, and that Newton extended their application to the planets by observing the fall of an apple. But if so, like many other myths, they are truer than history. The only motions we know are those close around us: and, while it is marvellous how they can be extended, we should never forget that it is only an extension of what is around us. Here motion is never alone, but is accompanied by much else, our own interference in particular, without which all science would be a closed book. But when motion is removed to the heavenly bodies, we know absolutely nothing about it except that it obeys the laws of motion. Then, having been stripped bare by removal into the otherwise unknown, it was brought back naked to explain the earth and all the fullness thereof, in a way so simple and complete and level to what we might do by our own understanding, that people only needed the help of a few large and learned words like "epiphenomenon" and "psycho-physical parallelism" to explain mechanically the very thoughts and interests by which alone we can know anything or deal with it in any way, in flat contradiction to daily experience and in a way to reduce to absurdity everything, and in particular our own minds, without which we could know nothing, not even this theory.

That we should discover from the order which rules about us, even were it only the mechanical part, what rules in all the inconceivable vastness of space, is very wonderful, but this does not justify us in taking, even from so amazing a journey, what has been reduced on it, only by our ignorance, to an abstraction, to determine either the nature or the limits of that from which it set out.

Modern Physics now extends its views by reasons of a mathematical kind, not by mechanism of a physical nature. But to bring even this back stripped by our ignorance of everything except the mere idea would again be to make an abstraction the measure of reality: and perhaps the greatest progress in modern Physics is that even the material world—if such a description is still permissible—has become for it so much more wonderful that it no longer encourages any such all-embracing infallibility.

It may be a delusive custom, as Butler says, to substitute imagination for experience, but it is a still more delusive custom to substitute argument, without any imagination of the possibilities beyond it, for humble readiness to learn from all experience. Perhaps the only real use of speculation is to remind us that the possibilities are as vast as they are varied.

Against similar arguing in religion I have spent still more energy than on this kind of arguing against it, but I now see that this also depends on the same use of argument sending our experience into the unknown, where ignorance reduces it to an abstraction, and then bringing it back stripped of its perplexities and uncertainties and so made infallible by its very nakedness, in order to rule out life's irreducible perplexities. This is not confined to science but is equally used by what we may call a Process Philosophy and an Omnipotence Theology.

On this earth and in our experience, we never find God's power working alone in independence of all that works with it and in particular our own co-operation. We do not find unity apart from what we are led to see united, or wisdom apart from seeking guidance. But when we abstract them from earth and send them up to heaven, where our ignorance unclothes them of all relations, nothing hinders us from calling unity The One and bringing it back naked and alone to reduce all difference to illusion, to *Maya*. So also the foresight and prevision, which we only see working amid earth's uncertainties and difficulties, we may transfer to heaven, where our ignorance sets them alone as omniscience and omnipotence and then bring them back simply as the fiat of the Absolute to explain all doings and all designs as either process or predestination. Neither is of grace, for it is not grace unless it win the heart, but is only power which breaks what will not bend. But, instead of spending our breath arguing against the blight of such contentions, we ought to see that all argument about infallibilities is just such abstraction of truths from their place in life, in which alone we deal with them.

Though maintained in the name of what is objective, thorough and practical, and, above all, theocentric, it is subjective, remote, anthropocentric. And yet, men in their desire to transfer the burden of their responsibility, continue to hanker after some infallibility isolated from the perplexities of human thought and the weakness of human purpose: and now that the ancient infallibilities of Church and Scripture seem to be tottering, they betake themselves to deifications which do not seem to rest on anything but lack of humour.

From the conviction that the fear of the Lord is the beginning of wisdom and that, to the end, duty is the only way our bleared eyes can discern or our feeble steps travel, the poet can extend his faith and say of duty:

"By thee the eternal heavens are fresh and strong."

But we may not argue back from what we take the eternal heavens to be to a duty which has its quality from an actual situation, with ourselves and our neighbours in it. Again we can reason with the prophets, from finding amid calamity that no evil finally overcomes good, to one righteous God omnipotent. But we cannot argue from that to determine any actual situation. We may reason, with Jesus, from the assurance that even the hairs of our head are numbered, to the Providence which orders the universe. But we cannot from an abstract idea of Providence argue to what it ought to appoint for us.

Moral and spiritual realities, like physical, we may extend to help us to realise that we live in an ordered world, and can believe it to be of wise love. But to introduce the infinite worlds to determine our religion here is only to import ideas of greatness where they do not belong.

Experience is a dialogue, whereby we learn as we ask the right questions and appreciate the right answers. This means being both humble and alert: and there is no worse preparation for profitable dialogue than a mind school-mastering everything by dialectic. And is the product of much that we call culture anything else?

CHAPTER IV

FINALITIES

WHEN honesty is reduced to the negative content of not believing anything that might possibly be mistaken and not doing anything that might possibly be folly, it is easy to find peace by confining attention to the obvious, restricting action to the materially insistent, and cultivating the sense of being emancipated persons of the superior company of the enlightened. Then, should serenity ever be darkened

> "by a sense sublime
> Of something far more deeply interfused,"

this can be dismissed as the shadow of superstition.

But anything worthy either to be thought or done has been found only by pushing out into the unknown, led forward only by a dim, yet persistent if vague, sense of right direction. As this kind of honesty is always facing the unknown and the undone, it is necessarily humble, and its fear is never of making mistakes, but of missing the highest and the best, in pursuit of which it is ever ready to follow the dimmest intuition of truth and the faintest aspirations after righteousness. Such honesty cannot fail to be concerned, first and last, with what stirs the mind to be ever reaching out beyond itself by reverence and ever seeing farther heights to be scaled. But while this settles the concern of honesty with religion, it does not determine what is honesty within it.

No other sphere is so liable to misuse. Religious professions provide the largest scope for hypocrisy; religious creeds for enslaving the mind to forms; religious duties for what may be fanciful or fanatical. This is no more proof that religion is either unreal or unprofitable than the growing of weeds disproves the existence or value of good soil. Religion has the mightiest of all sanctions for its claims, which is that they are sacred. In response to the obligation of what is sacred all heroic, self-denying service of good has been given: but, just because the sacred is the highest of all claims, it can be most abused.

Yet the problem of why God suffers evil is not confined to what is high. Is He not as much the ruler of the material world as of the spiritual? Why then should He not be committed to preventing abuse in the one as much as the other? If He should have prevented a wrong and did not, the principle of responsibility is not affected by its being small or great. The insistent question, therefore, is why God permits abuse of His good gifts in any sphere.

This is still a question of religion, because the possibility of such abuse arises from man's power to control and direct events according to his own purpose; and this, I have elsewhere maintained, he did by means of religion.[1] Reverence lifted up his mind above mere material impression, and the demand of the sacred gave him footing amid the flux of incident and the fleeting appeals of sense, and so provided him with an intellect which could seek permanent and real relations amid the customary sequence of happenings and a will which could set a course and not merely drift with the

[1] *The Natural and the Supernatural.*

veering winds of desire. Only when man could thus
alter the conditions given him could he use personal
enterprise for self-will and personal property for self-
interest: and, then only, could he really abuse either
nature or human nature.

Here we have the great watershed of views of religion.

Seeing what man has done with this power, is it not
the supreme lapse from innocence named the Fall and
rightly described as trying to be like gods? What is it
but using heaven's light to bury the nose in every filth,
as Mephistopheles says? Is it not then a pure abuse of
religion? And is not the right use of true religion just
to lead man back and restore him to the Eden of a
recovered calm and innocent acceptance of an un-
disturbed world?

Not only in theory, but in practice, much earnest
religion has taken this view. Pantheism mainly rests on
it, and all the pantheistic forms of Mysticism. Asceti-
cism is rarely for discipline, but is used as a way of
escape from distracting desires and burdensome relations
and responsibilities of possessions and complications of
the works of man. Agriculture has been forbidden,
nominally as a wounding of God's earth, but really as
the source of interference with things as they are and
the chief beginning of the burden of making them different. And in our day, when we have come to mean
by Humanism, not the fanning into flame of the Divine
spark in man, but that there is nothing higher than
man himself and nothing stronger than his might, have
we not reached the final impiety, and if religion has any
haven of peace to offer us, is it not in ceasing altogether
from concern with man whose breath is in his nostrils?

Or is the true failure in not carrying on with loyalty

and consecration the work religion has begun? Is the real world in which God has placed us to be measured by what ought to be and our real selves by what we ought to become, with the actual only as means for attaining them? Then the business of religion has to do not only with renouncing the world and denying ourselves in order to go beyond them, but also with using them as the necessary means for going beyond them; and the supreme error in religion is seeking finality either in renunciation of the actual or in contentment with it.

The question which goes deepest into the whole problem of our perplexing and troubled life is just whether, when we are face to face with God, we are dealing with final aims or with infinite. The answer, on either view, is mystery, but in the former case, the mystery is the perversity of man's doings; in the latter it is the manifold wisdom of God. In the former we think we know God's plan and the perplexity is that man is not made to follow it; in the latter God's purpose is beyond our knowing, but, as He is not content to achieve it except through the imperfect freedom of His children, the only evil He will not permit is stagnation in our own finalities. So long as, though faint, we pursue, even searching blind alleys of error and sin may be progress.

There are specially three finalities in which men have ever sought to find rest. They are Fixed Organisations, Fixed Ideals and Fixed Theologies.

First, Fixed Organisations

It is amazing that, with any knowledge of the past, any form of the State should be regarded as final. Yet the more rigid it becomes, and, therefore, the more exposed to being broken, the more those who order it hold it to be final and eternal. As before, the shades of mighty empires in the past will some day greet the present in Hades with the old cry, "Art thou also become like one of us!" And even while they last, the real end they serve may be the opposite of what the makers of them conceive.

Of our own religious order, when anyone is appointed like Jeremiah, to root up and to pull down, we are apt to think, like his contemporaries, that, seeing we take it to be God's particular business to keep it right, such action is mere profanation.

It may be our business to keep these organisations as secure and effective as we can, as they may give, for a time, needed shelter on man's long dangerous journey. Moreover, the more they have in them of spiritual purpose and freedom to follow it, the longer they will last. Yet, as they are no more than temporary means to infinite ends, they belong to the fashions of this world which ultimately pass away: and all we can pray for is that they may fade gradually and fruitfully into the next, and not have to be plucked up and pulled down in calamity, to make way for the new sowing and planting of something a little nearer to the order of the family of God. And this is as true of organised Churches as of organised States, even if, the need of them being greater and the spiritual basis of them securer, they may be more enduring.

Second, Fixed Ideals

Even if State or Church be beyond us to organise according to plan, have we not to organise our own lives according to a standard or ideal?

Most people in the last generation would have regarded it as indecent to be asked what was their ideal of life, for was it not fixed by standards above doubt or even discussion? And though we have ceased to regard any question as indecent, there is even to-day quite a large company who would have a nice set of formulas with which to answer. But the general dissatisfaction with the old answers appears from the way wisdom on the subject falls from the press as leaves in Vallambrosa, for, alas, leaves fall abundantly only when the life is stagnant and then they are dry.

The most notable effect is to help people to realise that they never had an ideal of life since about fourteen, when it was perhaps not higher than mine, which was to ride a horse bare-backed and steer a boat in a gale. After that age life became too complicated, too uncertain, too subject to change for keeping to any fixed mark. As problems turned up, we had to do our best to solve them, as situations occurred we had to do our best to meet them, as people came to depend on us we had to do our best to help them. If we ever entered on some larger undertaking, it was because opportunity challenged us. If we even imagined we had some kind of message to our fellows, it was because thought came and insisted on being uttered. Our best was just following glimpses of what appeared to be the higher way, with good company in all who keep on facing upward, however the track they follow differ from ours.

No fixed code is ever so hard that we could not have more success in keeping it, because, being a fixed mark, it is not for ever moving before us. But how can it be our business or the business of any director of our souls to fix ideals and formulate ends, if the measure is God's purpose not ours? If the goal set before us is what eye has not seen, we cannot determine it by experience; if ear has not heard it, we cannot fix it by tradition; if it is beyond all imagination, it cannot be determined by speculation. Then the question of all honesty in thought and action concerns following on to know the Lord, and, how that is to be endeavoured is a large part of the question before us.

Perhaps the only abiding gain in history has been the moving forward of human ideals, and our best gain from life the moving forward of our own. But, then, the last evil would be fixing them by narrow rules and regulations.

Third, Fixed Theologies

Even if we can have no finality about aught else, must we not have it about God? Yet is there any subject more than theology concerning which God has more confounded the wisdom of the wise and brought to nothing the understanding of the prudent?

Perhaps the greatest example of fixing theologies has been the early creeds settled as mysteries of an infallible Church. Like the laws of the State, they were to be received, as given, understanding and approval being irrelevant. For this the reason was that, in the chaos of the fall of the Roman Empire, the Church, in its efforts to restore order, had become a State.

To this we cannot deny some historical necessity. But historical necessities do not establish eternal truth. They only belong to the discipline of law, which is a school-master to lead us to the liberty which is in Christ Jesus. Wherefore, just because it was a State order and not the order of the family of God, it could not for ever go unquestioned.

Still more illuminating for us, is what took place when it was questioned.

What replaced at the Reformation the authority of the Visible Church was the doctrine of the Divine Sovereignty, exercised by predestination, election and absolute decree. This was by no means confined to Calvin. The domination of God over the slavery of the human will was as much the faith of Luther as of Calvin, though, as Luther's views were more modified by his followers than Calvin's, Lutheranism does not afford as clear an example as Calvinism.

What was great in Calvin was his belief that all trust in man is a broken reed and that there is no security save in God, but that, with this, nothing is impossible. Nor is there other immovable foundation for a faith able to support, in any crisis and against any foe, the cause of liberty. The expectation that freedom can be sustained by the natural desire to choose our own form of happiness ignores the fact that oppression and the love of domination can always be sure of reaching the point where faithfulness can be made more unhappy than surrender.

What was wrong was not this faith, but the direct way in which it was realised and the finality of creed, as well as of organisation, which was expected from it. In short it was expected to do, in somewhat the same external way, what had been looked for before from an infallible Church.

Of this the burning of Servetus was a mark. That so much has been made of it, shows how unique it was. But you cannot burn people by the sanction of a faith, even the surest, which is only of conscience of truth and righteousness. It requires an external, almost mechanical authority, belonging more to a State than a fellowship. Hence the action was a survival from the old authoritative Church, and assumed some similarity of fixed belief, and fixed organisation, and the reason for the assurance was thought to be secured by the doctrine of election, which seemed to guarantee the right reading of Scripture as infallible Divine legislation, a clear-cut plan of salvation, and a mechanical assurance of unity and order, almost, indeed, everything an authoritative Church had been before.

The value for the time is not difficult to see. Its simple and mechanical directness was an almost visible ark of the covenant: and if instead of this going before them, there had been a vision of all the doubt and division through which men would be led, would they ever have ventured on the long journey through the wilderness?

What happened is further instructive. When it became plain that neither creed nor order would remain a finality, those who still kept their faith in the fixed leading of God became still more rigidly Calvinistic, while those who did not became more Arminian and fell back on some kind of reconstruction of the authority of the Visible Church.

Yet it was not the liberty which is in Christ, but a temporary, if necessary, imposition of law, the business of which is to lead us to that liberty, not to keep us in tutelage.

The essential difference can be seen, if we compare Calvin with Paul. Paul's faith also is that all things are of God, and not in any way of man, and there is a superficial resemblance to this in their views of election.

Yet, for all that, there is a fundamental, transforming unlikeness. Calvin found mystery and perplexity in life, but none in God; and so was able to fall back directly on God's sovereignty, with all things being so because God wills them to be so. Then God's whole mind and purpose could be put into definite statements and precise definitions with His plan of salvation mapped out in black, straight, unmistakable lines. Sin is any want of conformity unto, or transgression of, the law of God; justification is a legal transaction, whereby these transgressions are legally condoned; sanctification is wrought out gradually afterwards, by Divine help, which, being thus isolated, can only be conceived mechanically.

There is none of Paul's deepest conviction that life is so dark a mystery because God is love with an infinite purpose, which we poor sinful mortals, even with all His help in Jesus Christ, see at best in broken glimpses and guess at best as an unsolved riddle. In short, for the Apostle, the one great mystery is just God.

Out of this comes the difference from Calvin in his conception of election. As touching the gospel, there may, for reasons of human perversity and reasons beyond our knowing, be present failure; but as touching election, we can be assured of a love which does not accept failure. Thus the Apostle has no finalities of creed or conduct or organisation, any more than his Master, but those who live in the fellowship of the Spirit are led by him, while Calvin's are all finalities.

Perhaps the sad story of man's whole history is that he would rather "have bondage with ease than strenuous liberty" and that this is just what life is appointed to disturb.

CHAPTER V

A PARABLE

"RENOUNCING the hidden things of dishonesty"
is the necessary beginning of all search for truth,
but if it be merely negative—unconcerned with
what is best worth knowing, unresponsive to what is
best worth appreciating, unadventurous in what is best
worth doing—it will never lead on to the discovery that
life's meaning is beyond the seen and its end beyond the
fleeting. For this, even an honesty, limited by rules of
logic, taste and behaviour, would be as though the
ancient mariners had hoped to explore the globe by
never going beyond their charts. Like them, we have
to use our charts as far as they serve, but our own task
only begins where they fail. In all our highest endeavour
we must fare forward in the right direction, as far as we
know it, to meet difficulties known and unknown, not
with mere grim determination but with a high and
cheerful glory in the adventure.

Such have been the great spiritual even as the great
material pioneers: and though they have made it easier
to follow, yet, as there are, no more in the spiritual
world than in the sea, fixed tracks to be kept to blindly,
we can follow only as a like spirit sustains us. Even
material conquests are not kept by slackness, but are
only truly possessed by seeking to use them to ever
higher ends; and spiritual possessions we inherit only as
we employ them for advancing in the adventure which

finds in each day's duty somewhat of the purpose of eternity.

This is the essential quality of faith: and, while faith in God may be more conscious of a higher object, it is not different in spirit and quality from the temper of patient hope and joyous adventure by which all life's possibilities have been made actual. Moreover, it is the same in that what we make out of life depends largely on how we meet failures, limitations and distresses, and above all our own errors and even our own sins. Also it is the same in that our success depends on our fellowship with others, trusting them and giving them reason to trust us, so that, in some dim way, this faith works in all spheres by love, if love mean understanding, appreciation and loyalty, for bitterness is blindness and blundering in every sphere.

Just as the creatures that came out of the slime developed lungs to prove the possibility of the dry land, and creatures that ventured above it developed wings to prove the possibilities of the air, so those, who came out of comfort and slackness and timidity and custom to follow higher calls, developed the aspirations, the insight, the sensitiveness, the enlightenment, the conscience to prove the possibilities of the world of spirit.

All this we are apt to think of as merely human, whereas we have no right to think of even the lowest life as apart from spiritual purpose and spiritual aid. Even the lowest perception is not a mere mechanical vibration of atoms, but requires, from the beginning, some freedom of response, the demand for which increases as the perception deepens in meaning. With religion this becomes a conscious experience as meaning from spirit to spirit: and when we recognise this relation as personal, we should mean by it that God's greatest way of giving is through ourselves, that, while we do nothing worthy except in Him, He does nothing effective except through us. Moreover, it is this reciprocity which makes anything spiritual—what is merely imposed, whether by direct act or by process, never being more than mechanical.

Yet, though no spiritual good can be merely given and continue spiritual, God is constantly thought of as absolute fiat or resistless process. Then, on the one hand, honesty seems to demand either that we dismiss the whole business of religion because God is not a proposition legally proved, a ruler irresistibly omnipotent, a revealer of exact information; or, on the other, to maintain that He is all this, with complete independence of our thoughts and our insight. One has the self-approval of exclusive honesty from disbelief and the other from belief, yet both are not only from the same conception of God as abstract omniscience and omnipotence, but from the same impatient, rationalist temper which works with dogmas of finality.

More and more I seem to see that we make much or little out of life according to the temper in which we face it, and perhaps honesty is at bottom a question of temper, and temper a question of honesty. But it is a temper applied to religion in life, and, not primarily at least, to philosophical questions about God or historical questions about the Bible.

Seeing how Jesus obviously used parables as vivid teaching to simple people, the saying attributed to Him that He spoke in parables that outsiders should not understand the mystery of the Kingdom may not be genuine. Yet, as it is only a quotation from Isaiah, where it means not understanding but the illusion of it, even though the parables are obviously intended to make truth plain to simple people, the saying might still have the fitting meaning that He would not give truth in general statement, but would keep it in the midst of life's daily tasks and trials, with the necessity of kindness, loyalty and sincerity in all common relations, for the genuine reception of it. At all events, the parables speak of religion, not in the synagogue or the temple, but amid digging and sowing and buying and selling, and children's play and mixing with shady characters. The assumption of it all apparently is that, if we do not find God in events as they happen and what we can do with them and among men as they are and what we can bring out of them, we shall not find Him anywhere, yet therein we shall not fail if we are humbly in earnest to discern the best and have a human friendliness to call it forth.

This concerns not merely honesty about religion, but what is much further reaching—honesty within it, the vital concern not being about having religion, but about the kind of religion we have.

The higher world can be misused as well as the lower; and the ways of misuse are similar in both spheres, being either in the way of hardness or of softness, like a touch which is sensitive to all surfaces but shrinks from none.

To save ourselves from degenerating into generalities, we shall speak of it as the parable of "Calling a Spade a Spade", though it may rather be a parallel than a parable.

The spade is the essential elementary tool whereby man has dug out earth's possibilities, from his patch of grain to the pinnacles of his cathedrals.

This was not done by seeing the end from the beginning and fashioning vast schemes for attaining it, but by honest digging with a real spade at what presented itself to be done, and by pushing, through the immediate task, to something ever higher, by an inspiration, guidance and perseverance in man's soul which was at least akin to faith, hope and love.

In this temper it was just a spade, to deal with chalk and gravel and clay as they presented themselves, not as enemies to be vanquished, but as friends to be persuaded to display their bounty, whose ways we must learn and on whose promise we must wait with cheerful, hopeful, honest industry. Nor is it merely benefit to ourselves that has accrued. All pleasant and profitable kindly fellowship has also been won in the toil and the profit of this service. Thus the treasures of thought, character and loyalty have been as much dug out of the earth as coal or iron.

But when earth's possibilities are not realised in this temper, we may err on either hand. The spade may become a "shovel", with an adjective which indicates slavish toil to earn a livelihood and brutal encounters to defend it; or an "implement", with an adjective which indicates the purpose of making life "a garden enclosed, with beds of spices and feeding among lilies". To call it the former is to take life to be one long encounter with nature and human nature to hold our own against them and wring what we want out of them. To call it the latter is to think we can ignore all but our own enclosed patch of fruitful soil, which will provide life's amenities with mere pleasant, health-giving recreation.

You can have a science of the spade. Is it not a remarkable combination of the forces of potential and kinetic energy, bearing, as mass and muscle, on a sharp cutting-edge, with the principle of the lever applied to the resisting forces of cohesion and gravitation?

You can also have a philosophy of the spade. Did it not lay the foundation of man's development as a tool-using animal: and does not M. Bergson trace the development of man's intellect as an instrument for cutting up the world to suit his convenience to his use of tools, and is not the primary tool the spade?

You might also have a song of the spade, of its beautiful, cheerful, human achievement, as it grows sharp and bright in the hands by use, and gives the satisfaction of something profitable actually done.

But the really decisive matter is the religion of the spade, for all these tempers have their religion.

We can also have a science, a philosophy and a poetry of religion, but in the end it is the temper in which we, as it were, dig into it in life and for nobler living, that determines what our religion is and what it does.

The higher world can be misused as well as the lower: and that in either way of hard brutality or sentimental softness. Its tremendous sanctions can be invoked for brutalities and slavishness, if we are brutal and domineering; or to enable us to float away into a world of elysiums and sentimentalities and mystical withdrawals from life's burdens and distresses and obligations, if we love emotion more than reality. It is a world which has often been cultivated with very bloody shovels, with human sacrifices and the scaffold and the stake; and also with soft, sentimental, magically impressive horticultural implements.

Yet through all the ages and in all religions, there have been the honest people, who, in their hearts, and with their hands as well as their tongues, faced reality as it met them, and dug in it to discover what ore is hid in its veins or what harvest it is fitted to produce, or what material it has for structures of utility and beauty. They did honest digging, as they dealt with all life in humility and hope and faith and patience, to discover what is truly sacred, or, in other words, what is God's mind and what victories He will have us win in the earth. Thereby, men have discovered the ore of noble character, the harvest of kindly and self-forgetting service, and have reared sublimer temples of beauty and reverence than the cathedrals. And this they have done as they called a spade a spade, working with joy and hope and patience, and shunning the brutalities of violence on the one hand and evasive sentimentalities on the other. Thus they discovered that the real, deep, hidden possibility even of what is, is what ought to be, and learned better what truly ought to be.

Even in the lowest religion there is this search and some beginning of discovery. At first, men could only conceive the spiritual materially through life and then through a semi-material soul, and they related it to blood and birth and the produce of their fields. But they found thereby a sense of a deeper reality both within and without. And the people who faced all reality honestly, in humble, hopeful willingness to learn, and had the courage of faith to venture through the worst on what they saw to be highest, grew in spiritual insight and came into fuller possession of the true meaning and blessing of the world. Even for the religion of Jesus, it is not irrelevant that He was a carpenter, shaping the stateliest of earth's products into humble utensils for human service, or for His way of thinking of it that His favourite illustration of it was from the growth of the fields. Just by this concern with the common interests of common people He wrought the victory of honest religion in the earth as no other.

And we can say more even of Jesus than that He wrought the victory of honest religion in the earth as no other. For the most part, He met only the most ordinary people, but consider what He found in them and what He had to say to them. His teaching dealt only with such common events as any of us could meet any day, but how deep it penetrated and how high it soared! No doubt He was inspired continually by His vocation to manifest the Rule of God, but He found the Rule for Himself by the events that came to Him. Nor did He need great events to make them great occasions. It is sometimes said that He planned His crucifixion. But what we read in the Gospels is that this and all His life came to Him as He manifested His loyalty to His Father's will, not by appointing His own way, but by following, as it was appointed, all life just as it came, and not evading even its worst brutalities. He looked all iniquity in the face and had terrible things to say about it, but He bore Himself as one who knew that God's forbearance is His appeal to the unthankful and the evil and that this is His perfection, into which we enter as we are like Him.

His final victory is the Cross. Yet there is nothing else about which we can be more what He was not—hard or sentimental.

The more obvious misapprehension is the way of evasive sentimentality. The crucifixion is softened down into an impressive religious ceremonial and the cross is turned into an ecclesiastical ornament. Thus religion becomes the refined taste which turns its eyes from life's brutalities and passes by on the other side. But the actual cross was a ghastly instrument of torture, the invention of man's horrible cruelty, and the actual crucifixion was an agonizing execution as a criminal, which was a hypocritical and vile, as well as a brutal, perversion of justice, with its chief cause bad religion.

Yet the other way is also plain. It is seen even in the artists, and that, not merely in the brute violence of a Caracci, for Ruskin complains that even the great Italian artists too often wallow in blood. There is nothing of being more than conqueror, nothing but the mere agonizing victim: and the moral would be that naked violence, clothed in power, rules the world.

Moreover, there can be a mixture of these seeming opposites in a use of the Cross as a means of self-pity, whereby to think of ourselves as, like Jesus, beautiful souls the world despises and rejects and handles shamefully.

But the Cross is victory over all ills—agony, the wrath of man, ignominy, death—and the turning of them into peace, and joy and spiritual possession, because our Lord met all brutality knowing what it was, yet having no part in it.

We have still even in Christ's name a good deal of crude material shaking of people over the pit, of imposition of traditions and of hard respectabilities; and we have still more of sentimentalities, ceremonialisms, and churchy religion, which tithes mint, anise and cummin and neglects the weightier matters of the law. But there never was a time when we had greater need for people, never hard on the one hand or sentimental on the other, who will go on asking the old question, What in this perplexing world is God's real purpose? and in cheerful patience follow on to know and serve it only. They are the only people who rightly pray: "Our common Father who art in the heavenly things, let man's soul be lifted up to revere all that is included in Thy name, Thy kingdom come, whatsoever other kingdoms disappear, and Thy will be done in earth as in heaven, with whatever agony we may have to renounce our own", which is the only prayer of honest dealing with all life's facts and possibilities.

Of this too, when we stand back from it and are living on the fruits of other people's religion, we can have a science and a philosophy, and they may serve useful purposes of knowledge. But we must not suppose that either can do the business of religion. Science is concerned with simplification and working back to beginnings; religion is concerned with aspirations, intuitions and ultimate ends. Philosophy is concerned with our understanding of the universe; yet if it were capable of knowing the whole universe, religion would still be asking what God means to make of the infinite possibility of increasing purpose, and how by God's help and guidance we are to help towards its realisation. Religion is not a scheme of the Cosmos, not even a plan for our world or even an ideal for our lives, yet is continually seeking in the events that come to us the things that excel as God shows their excellence.

In religion we must be as bold, as free, as honest, as prepared to face all realities as in science or philosophy. Slavery to tradition, fear of inquiry, submission to institutions are not religion but the want of it, not faith but unbelief. The difference is only in the sphere in which honesty is exercised, religion being the sphere in which we are ever reaching out beyond what eye has seen. Science and philosophy have their place, and man's restless mind will ever try to think things together. But religion has ever been the creative force in history, and man's central interest must ever be in reaching forward and upward toward a world not yet realised. That is religion, and man will not cease to be religious till he is satisfied and no more stakes all, his life included, on what has not even yet entered into his heart to conceive. Yet this too is a world in which, by violence or evasiveness, by want of the humility which learns and the patience which pursues, we can miss our way. And is there any other way of finding our true bearings than the spirit of Christ and His reconciliation to all God requires as well as all He appoints, without resentment and without evasion?

CHAPTER VI

PROPHETIC REVELATION

As the way we have just considered seems to be between extremes, would it not be pleasanter, as well as more erudite, to call it the Via Media, rather than the Narrow Way? As this requires something of cultured piety, there might still be few that find it, but would they not be the choicest company?

And, at its best, the temper of nothing too much does provide something fine and gracious, which is ill replaced by the vulgarity to which extremes are as the breath of life, which threatens in our day to become the favourite form of hypocrisy, even though hypocrisy may seem to be the only evil it ever wishes to escape and honesty the one virtue of which it is assured. It defies ancient taboo and modern Mrs Grundy, boasts of saying what it thinks however it offend, admires brazenly what it fancies, however little admirable, does unashamedly what it likes, however inconsiderate, and disapproves of nothing except repression. But hypocrisy is deceiving ourselves and trying to deceive others by playing to the gallery; and the kind of ostentation, whether of piety or impiety, which is regarded as effective, depends on the actor's view of the taste of his audience: and, if, in the process, he become so identified with his part that its unworthiness receives his own approbation, so much the more is it hypocrisy. Then he can have a smugger approval of himself for having neither reserve nor self-repression than Mrs Grundy ever conferred on the most approved demureness of bearing or respectability of behaviour. As it all depends on the fashion of one's circle, there may be conventional ungodliness and licence as readily as conventional godliness and propriety. Yet, though conventionality is evil, we all depend in some degree on conventions, and it is not unimportant that they should have in them something of the golden mean.

The name Via Media, for a religion which stresses this, is specially associated with one Church. But most educated people in most Churches tend to take it: and they are all in the same danger that their education should be in the Laodicean temper which shuns the heights and shirks the depths which give meaning and value to experience.

Yet the remedy for the religious limitation of the genial person is not another limitation to the way of the austere, to be walked in mainly by repressions and revolt against amenities generally, and natural gaiety of spirit in particular. As life's realities are often sad and self-command has often to be stern, hardness easily masquerades as strength. Hence to many austerity appears the very hall-mark of religion, and to say with Isaac Walton, "If thou be a sour-complexioned man I disallow thee to be a judge in the matter", would seem undisguised worldliness. Yet, by few things more than hardness, and not least with ourselves, do we miss life's best blessings, for to fail to respond to life's joys and see even in the darkest distresses the joy of the Lord is to miss the light which shines on to victory and peace.

Nor though we may disastrously err from it on either

hand, is the narrow way to be kept by balancing like a child performing on a paling, as though safety lay in anxious responsibilities and meticulous avoidances and observances. The way is narrow not to burden our ease or check our freedom, but simply because it is the one direct road to the goal.

This difference of view regarding the way, presents the vital question to our honesty of whether our religion is primarily a gospel or primarily an ethic. Does it merely demand honesty from us, or is it such a dealing of God's grace with us that we cannot but be open and manifest in His sight? In other words, does our religion first of all make demands to be met by effort and determination, or is it supremely the inspiration of faith in a gracious purpose for which all things work graciously?

We cannot answer this question merely by saying that God gives and we receive, for it would not be grace were it mere giving and receiving.

We may give, like the unrighteous judge, to save trouble, and receive, like the importunate widow, as nothing more than our due. Right giving requires both love and wisdom, and right receiving esteem for the giver and responsibility for the gift. The best teaching is help to teach ourselves, and the best moral aid help to stand on our own feet. The ideal giving is a good and wise father's subordination of all his giving to making his son an independent and responsible person, and the ideal receiving for the son to prove himself worthy in an independent manhood.

If God be a father in this sense and if this is how He gives, He can no more simply dictate His revelation than He can simply pour in His grace. God's revealing

and man's discovering will not be opposites but necessary one to the other. God has not truly revealed till
man discovers; and it is no true discovery unless it be
what God has revealed. The organ of revelation is the
prophet, but the prophet is just the person who most
depends on God for what he knows; and though it is
by consecrated insight that he is attuned to it, this also
is not apart from God. And for the reception of the
prophet's message we have to pray that all the Lord's
people be prophets, for we cannot be built upon the
foundation of the apostles and prophets by submissive-
ness to tradition, but only by being in some measure
ourselves apostles and prophets. Then and then only
can we abandon all idea of compulsion as inconsistent
both with real reception of God's truth and the liberty
of His children.

We should not think that God never revealed anything except what is our Scriptures. Zoroaster was a
great hero of religion when he said, Do thy tasks and live
thy life and neither fear nor worship the powers of evil.
Buddha was another when he said that the tremendous
thing in life is the moral consequences of desire. But as
the religion of both was arrested at the legal idea of
material good to him who does good, the religion of
the former degenerated into ceremonies to evade the
consequences, and that of the latter into emptying life
of value and purpose by eliminating desire.

Therefore, the essential line of progress was in the
Hebrew prophets, because they taught that, even when
God renders to everyone according to his works, He
shows mercy. Thereby they laid the foundation for
victory over the repression of mere law on the one hand

and fear of ceremonial taboo on the other, and gave life meaning and value and purpose by lifting men's hearts towards faith in a love which is infinite at once in compassion and in the reach of its requirements.

Yet the prophets were not independent of their background and the whole Old Testament shows what this was. It was far below the prophetic teaching, whether on faith or morals. The sense of holiness was still confused with ceremonial cleanness, sacred obligation with custom in Israel, the Lord of Hosts with the national leader. Yet as the holiness was for absolute reverence, the sacred requirement for absolute obligation, and God alone for loyalty and service, though there was a dependence on material embodiments and rules and regulations which exposed to the danger of polytheism of the mind, for those who were reverent without hardness and loyal without evasion, the material was ever becoming more transparent with the spiritual and the spiritual ever more a unity for the heart and conscience. From them the prophets sprang as well as to them the prophets spoke. Yet, even in Israel, the prophets remained unique in the consistency with which, without outward bond or direction and solely by their own inspired insight, they moved towards a faith which was not mere intellectual monotheism, but the assurance of one wise righteousness in all and over all.

Like other early religions, Hebrew religion began with primitive ideas of sacrifice and priesthood and ceremonial law. To try to persuade ourselves, therefore, that all the Old Testament is revelation of eternal truth and permanent Divine legislation, is not even plausible honesty. The revelation was in the progress through the material to the spiritual. Therefore, though it was unique and no working of the merely natural, to separate God's guidance from man's honesty in seeking and following it, is a vain and foolish distinction. The distinction is between the chaff and the wheat. The chaff had its purpose. It was the necessary if temporary sheath. But when the grain is ready to be seed to the sower and bread to the eater, the next process is to winnow the chaff away. Thus, though Isaiah's religion doubtless came through those who felt in the material worship an ever more spiritual presence, when he heard the cry "Holy, holy, holy, is the Lord of Hosts: the whole earth is full of His glory", he could dispose of the anxious concern of his contemporaries with the merely ceremonial as "vain oblation". So also his contemporary Micah, though he also had his ancestry in those who through sacrifice had learned service, could proclaim that God requires nothing but to do justly and love mercy and walk humbly with Him.

Here then we discern that the human side of revelation is simplicity in the heart and loyalty in the life, without hardness and without evasion: and if God thereby led men out of material taboo and ancient superstition, it was no less His way of revealing, for being also of His patience with man's receiving.

But here it may be that you ask, "What does the word of God mean if we abandon all idea of compulsion except persuasion by such truth as man is able to receive? Under such conditions there can be no finalities; and what is revelation if not of finalities?"

All God's dealing with us should be revelation, and the special prophetic history, which we regard as

O   D revelation in a particular sense, is really the history of reconciliation, which is to say of so learning God's mind behind his rule that we can accept it without being tempted to deceive either ourselves or others. Yet this concerns what is true and not merely what is edifying: and the question is how do we know it to be true?

If the first and great commandment is "Thou shalt love the Lord thy God with all thy heart, and with all thy soul, and with all thy mind", and the second, "Thou shalt love thy neighbour as thyself", is like unto it, it is no commandment that could be enforced by anything apart from itself. Even to approach it is possible only as we live in one rule of God which draws out our devotion to Him and our service to man, by having no place for merely selfish ends. Yet this rule approves itself to us as the final reality only as we thus live in it. A law which hangs on this is no longer a law which outward authority could enforce. If it is still the law, it is turned by prophecy into a rule of God which appeals and does not merely command. It is law as Jesus fulfilled it by making it cease to be a law of commandments.

Like Jesus, the prophets observed the forms of worship of their time, but drew no authority from any recognised church or support from any recognised priesthood. They learned from one another, but only as it increased their insight and never in the dependence of disciples. In Hosea we already find the essential message of all the prophets, though their consistency was never by looking back on the past, but always by looking for an increasing vision of the truth. And, if we can learn from him with like freedom, it will reward us also to start from Hosea. The simple question is whether we are under the rule of the wise love of the Father which leads us on, or of a mechanically determined Fate which drives us forward: and it will carry us further to see the former faiths working in a human life than by merely raising the general problem. Of this the earliest, best, and most challenging presentation is that with which Hosea closes his prophecies. "Asshur shall not save us; we will not ride upon horses: neither will we say any more to the work of our hands, Ye are our gods: for in Thee the fatherless findeth mercy. I will heal their backsliding, I will love them freely."

What Hosea rejects is very modern if we put the name of almost any armed state for Assyria. On all outward showing the organised might of Assyria was irresistible and riding upon horses the terrible incarnation of it. Among his people, Hosea was almost alone in refusing to bow down to it. The conviction in which he stood was that not violence however armed, or wickedness however entrenched, but mercy and righteousness rule the world. Just because it was his own conviction won in face of the most overwhelming experience of outward disasters both in his public and private life and of the inward agony of a sensitive and sympathetic spirit, it is no mere speculative notion. A faith which could triumph over an evil that had wrecked his own home and a violence that was about to lay waste his country, for both of which his heart bled in anguish, deserves our regard as tried in all things and still sure.

His faith went against all appearances, and as it is precisely when all seems to be against us that we most need its support, no other faith is of value: and what is noteworthy about faith is that it usually is strongest when events are most hostile and the heart is most overwhelmed in sympathy and sorrow. All the prophets after him accepted Hosea's faith in face of the same overwhelming experience of public disaster and personal scorn and opposition.

Nor is this confined to Scripture. The harder the conflict the more prophetic souls have found peace and strength in the same convictions. This surely requires reflexion, and honest reflexion ought to consider whether it is not man's world being so much with us in comfort and possessions that hides from us God's world, and whether our own ignorance of His rule in it is due, not to its darkness, but to our own obliquity of vision and evasion of conflict.

If, as Hosea affirms, "the ways of the Lord are right", they should at least in some measure and in time show themselves, even by outward events, to be right. Nor has time wholly failed to confirm his assurance that "the just shall walk in them; but transgressors shall fall therein". Assyria was perhaps the most brutal and destructive incarnation of might the world ever saw, being able to "gather nations as one gathers eggs, and no one opened the mouth or cheeped". Yet no great nation ever vanished so utterly without leaving a wrack behind of anything to enrich mankind; while Hosea's own work not only determined the message and the method of all later prophecy, but is still challenging prophetic souls to inquire whether it applies to life, and, as Hosea thought, is proved by right living. If the ways of the Lord are of mercy and not of might, they are long ways, but if they are right, they must, in the end, be sure ways.

At all events, no other ways are sure, no profound reflexion being needed to see that the greatest domination of man is but a potter's vessel on time's angry flood. Is not Pascal right when he says that it was pardonable in a callow youth like Alexander to be swash-bucklering about, conquering the world, but Caesar had surely arrived at too mature an age for such frivolity?

Prophecy, in Isaiah, sees them as smoking stumps of burned-out firebrands: and to that they and all such as they come and with them the work of their hands to which, though extended by the machine and defended by the machine-gun, they said, Ye are gods.

This time will show, but in its welter, the prophetic message that in God the fatherless, the representative of all the helpless, finds mercy, and that He heals backsliding and loves freely, is hard to believe. Nevertheless, Hosea says we can know it to be true, if we follow on to know.

How this is done, Hosea himself tells us. "Who is wise, and he shall understand these things? prudent, and he shall know them? for the ways of the Lord are right, and the just shall walk in them; but transgressors shall fall therein"—"these things" meaning specially that the world is ruled by mercy and not by human domination.

Wisdom has come to have the cheap meaning of sagacity, and prudence of caution. But we may interpret Hosea by our distinctions of the overruling sense of the holy and the absolute demands of the sacred. What he means by wisdom is not sagacity nor learning nor ability. It is an understanding of life by sensitiveness to the appeal of the holy. If no feeling speaks to us except the sense of material good, how can we begin with any higher meaning in the world? No higher insight or value or purpose can dawn upon our spirits if, even in what the senses say to us, there is nothing above sense. Nor is there any final guidance except utter loyalty to truth and right just because they are sacred. Argument cannot help us, nay argument about the highest claims is itself dishonest. But, with a responsive spirit, weakness and error and even sin will not hinder light arising in the darkness.

Prudence here means the right application of what is of sacred requirement. It is what the Apostle Paul speaks of as practical discernment; which concerns the right uses of life guided by the absolute demands of the sacred. By wisdom we discern; by discriminating application we prove—"know" here meaning to be sure of: and we do so by seeing the ways of the Lord to be right, and judge right alone to be trustworthy, and not by either immediate or future profit. Therefore, no one can answer except for himself. In the end no one can say to his brother "Know the Lord" or lay down rules to guide his steps. Only direct knowing is knowledge and only doing from the heart is service.

But how are we to be truly honest concerning it? When have we exercised the wisdom which alone could discern and the practical application which alone can verify? If the real meaning of all things is God's mind and their real end God's purpose, can we expect to know this save by sensitiveness which enables us to see the next step and to see further by taking it? At our best we finite creatures could only be blear-eyed and of halting step, but surely we see wonders enough to assure us of greater beyond, and the blatant self-confidence that human knowledge covers it all and human uses embrace all its value is only purblind vanity. What men see in life and what they make out of it depends on the attitude they assume towards it: and the larger their expectation, the humbler their seeking, the more patient their knocking, the more their sympathy with human weakness and the greater their reverence for human goodness, the more life has for them of meaning, the higher its promise, the fuller its assurance of unfailing mercy and immeasurable truth. Then the more abounding all things are in present spiritual value the greater is the promise beyond. But, if the blindness we have is just from lack of utter consecration to seeing and doing, may we not sum it up as sin, and find that the end of all our reasoning with God is to have our eyes made willing at all costs to see and our wills at all sacrifice to follow on to know?

Yet we may not learn till the things wherein we trust for our security have proved to be deceitful mirages in the desert. Hence it is that, just when life is most distressing, it is most transparent and our vision clearest; while the times of our greatest darkness are the times of our ease. Hence too those who have most shown its power and who help us to faith were those of whom man's world was not worthy and who were paid the wages of poverty and opposition and ignominy for the greatest of all benefits, the inheritance of the fullness of God's own world.

CHAPTER VII

INSPIRATION AND CRITICISM

B<small>UT</small> if this is the concern of the higher honesty, what about the lower? Has it followed and supported the higher interest or been its rival? Has not the dust raised by it over questions of text and interpretation and authorship and history constantly obscured the higher vision? Just as many young people have been made incapable of reading Shakespeare with imagination and delight by the painful labours of Aldis Wright and Verity, so is not the Biblical critic, with his toilsome and not very literary or religious dissection both of the matter and letter of Scripture, to blame for the loss of spiritual appreciation of the Bible? When it becomes pabulum for erudition is there not danger of forgetting that it was written for the sympathetic understanding of ordinary religious people? Not only is criticism not everyone's business, but, if one remain just the sort of person for whose insight and appreciation the Scriptures were written, keeping as far from the theologian as the critic and maintaining an open mind, would he not probably take more out of them and be less mistaken about their essential message than either the theologian or the critic?

Usually, however, it is just for dogmatic reasons that criticism is denounced. Does not revelation require inspiration and inspiration carry with it accurate information, assured authorship, exact transmission?

What then can criticism be but impious desecration and the pursuit of it but deliberate malignity? Moreover, are not critics all at sixes and sevens, and has not the antiquarian sometimes proved them to be in error?

Nor is this all without some justification. The critic, being assured of loyalty to truth in his labours, is apt to forget how much, in so problematical a task, he is exposed to the shortcomings of human nature. The field offers large opportunities for being at the mercy of fashions of thought, for making erudite assumptions seem facts to build on, for giving false weight to opinions by repetition of echoes, and for mistaking the clever for the convincing. Uncertainties remain uncertainties however much argument be expended upon them, and, as with other opinions of specialists, we, who are not specialists, may know that they are wrong without knowing why.

Further, though not a valid objection from the literalist's point of view, there has been exaggeration of the importance of conclusions about integrity and authorship. If truth depend upon what is said, not on who says it, questions of authorship cannot be of the first importance; and if there has been any fusion of works by different authors, they have been usually put together to good purpose and to edification.

Nevertheless, it is pitiful to see good people turning an occasional refutation by the antiquarian into a charge of persistent perversity, and grasping at easily explained differences of opinion to discredit as an emissary of Satan the higher critic, when if the Bible were to them what they profess, they should not be afraid of anything vital in it being shaken.

If we ignore traditional interpretation and read with open mind, we cannot escape critical questions of our own; and if they be further raised for us from the outside it is not honesty to dismiss them on some dogmatic idea of inspiration. There are the same errors in the text as in other ancient documents, the same doubt about authorship and fusion of writings, the same melting of history back into tradition and tradition into myth, while the religion, if higher than elsewhere, is still coloured by the thoughts and practices of the time.

When this is seen to be met by blind conservatism, timidity and mental rigidity, it seems to justify the dismissal of the whole subject of the Bible as an outlived relic of antiquity and, with it, the whole business of religion as a superstition only to be accepted by those who do not know what intellectual honesty means.

Then we have the equally unedifying spectacle of gloating over every hint of myth and kinship with lower religions and indications of inconsistency and variety of authorship, in order to be able to look down upon religion and every other higher aspiration as if nothing ever shed the limitations of the hole of the pit from which it was digged.

Nothing is to be rejected because of human failure to rise to the height of its requirements. Blind conservatism, timidity and mental rigidity are common failings of human nature to be found in every sphere. Science has been arrested for centuries by dogmas built on theories as if they were facts, but this is no reason for rejecting science as a whole. Criticism itself has too frequently been at the mercy of fashions in thinking and has often hardened into dogma. But if that is no reason for rejecting criticism as a whole, neither is it for rejecting religion or even the Bible as a whole.

The real reason why criticism is accepted whole is the same as the reason why it is rejected whole. It is the same dogmatic assumption about revelation: that what is God's work is not man's and that what is man's work is not God's, that revelation is what God says, not what man hears, and that the way to know God's mind is to have no mind of our own. Thus opposite conclusions spring from the same dogmatic type of thinking, to which it would seem to be a contradiction in terms when the Apostle says, "Work out your own salvation with fear and trembling, for it is God that worketh in you" both the willing and the doing. Yet how could we will and do unless God had wrought in us the power; and why should He work it except to be exercised? Moreover, on this very matter of inspiration the Apostle adds that the spirits of the prophets are subject to the prophets, for God is not a God of confusion but of peace. Inspiration, this means, is not submission to a possession, but is for knowing God's order by our own insight and being sure of it by our own consecration: and only such knowing God is for salvation. To be inspired is not to cease to think, but to be helped to think to right purpose. Nor was there ever any body of men, more than the prophets, to whom utter dependence upon God gave more utter independence of men in thought as well as action. Nor is anyone a prophet who has not won like independence by like means. A prophet is precisely one whom the Lord takes with a strong hand and instructs not to walk in the way of this people, and not to be shadowed by their suspicions, or afraid with their fears.

It must, therefore, be a vain and foolish idea that we could be built on the apostles and prophets by mere subjection to their instruction and guidance, as if the way to see that what they say is true were to surrender the independence of mind whereby they saw it and of will whereby they proved it. Hence the folly of thinking that subjection is the ground of faith and the way of godliness.

This question of the verbal authority of Scripture is far from being new. No modern fundamentalism can ever have been so shocked by the most radical criticism as the devout Jews who regarded the Law as the most inspired of all writings, when told by the Apostle to the Gentiles that it was a mere leader of children to bring them to the liberty of the true teacher, and only of temporary value. And we have only gone a step further on the same road when we say that myth was a school-master to lead to the Law.

The Bible would only deserve all the enquiry devoted to it if it is great religious literature; and as such it should be treated with becoming reverence. Yet criticism may not allow its conclusions to be swayed even by reverence. This, as Butler says, would be a prejudice as much as anything else. In coming to conclusions criticism should be determined only by its own reasons—literary if literary, historical if historical.

Certain broad conclusions are then reasonably established. Like all early histories, the early history in the Bible was written by piecing together earlier chronicles, which were composed occasionally from records of some kind, but mainly from tradition. And though tradition may be much more reliable than the man whose memory depends on writings assumes, if history is only an imperfect record, tradition must be more so. Then behind tradition can only be myth, in which actual happenings may be reflected, but in a form not to be distinguished from imaginings.

An occasional triumph over the critic in which the antiquarian proves him to have pushed his scepticism too far has not undermined these general conclusions. What might with better reason be charged against him is readiness to accept every other explanation than the religious, which to the Scripture writers themselves is the only one of any consequence, and which, as a matter of fact, was of the first importance.

It would be easy to draw the conclusion, from some criticism at least, that the political motive was the only impulse of the time and the religious introduced by reflexion afterwards; that the prophets were astute, far-seeing politicians, not, as they themselves affirmed, persons wholly occupied with God's rule and His mind in all events; that the ritual and law were nothing more than a relic of early religion of a material and magical kind, wrought up for the unity of the nation and by the influence of the priesthood; that the history was common secular history told by pious historians, and the mythology the ordinary way of the primitive mind to think in story, as if in the Bible nothing more were thought through it than primitive phantasies.

But, if all the Bible were mythology, it would contain more real experience of religion than all the philosophies of religion. What is wonderful about the mythology of the Bible is the thought of God and the world and life, so different from all other mythologies. Though expanded and exalted by the later writers, it was not fundamentally altered; and as there was no outward authority to direct it, this keeping to one path would seem to show that they were led on by one consistent vision of reality.

The ritual and the commandments contained in ordinances, which together the Apostle calls the Law, were not very different in outward matters from many other early religions, and doubtless had their origin in a primitive feeling about sacred offerings and especially the blood-offering. Both mark a people still much dependent on the material sacred and ideas fixed in this association.

Only the great prophets rose with any freedom above the sacrificial and legal forms. But, through the prophets, these forms came to embody higher thoughts of the Divine and of a purity that was moral and of sin and righteousness which were of the heart. The prophets had turned law into liberty, and these again turned liberty into law. But while they could not maintain the prophetic progress by open vision, they made an important part of the prophetic message the heritage of the whole people and brought about the day Hosea hoped for, when Ephraim had no more to do with idols, but turned for ever from the ecstatic, sensuous worship around them, which was as debasing morally as it was idolatrous. Though the original inspiration was through specially endowed and consecrated individuals, the cult confirmed the prophetic idea of a nation specially called for a Divine purpose and gave a religious value to the whole Old Testament and not merely to the parts which we might regard as specially religious.

All progress has been by those called and endowed for it; and the significance of Israel for the knowledge of God and of His rule no doubt meant special gifts and experiences of special persons. Yet prophecy is not exalted, ecstatic, individual manifestations, but is an interpretation of experience for all to verify by insight and consecration. Nor is there any finality ever offered except ceaseless loyalty to the inexhaustible Divine purpose. Hence the honest people to whom it still commends itself are those who believe wholly in the eternal expansion of truth, seek with perfect heart the beauty of holiness, hunger and thirst after righteousness, and humbly and faithfully follow the highest God has given them to know. Religion speaks of faith, not courage, but faith is just inspired courage to follow the beckoning of the highest. Whatsoever human elements have been mixed with the receiving we can accept, not as part of the faith, yet as a necessity of man's part in believing.

How great the Old Testament revelation of God was appears in the way Jesus started from it; and how great His revelation of the Father was appears in how far it went beyond what was reached by even the greatest of the prophets.

CHAPTER VIII

THE FATHER

IT has been said that Jesus speaks of the Father and it is religion; theology speaks of God and it is only cosmology. But this depends on what we mean by religion and by cosmology. If religion means edifying and comforting piety, it is singularly absent from both the life and the teaching of Jesus; whereas, if cosmology mean how the world is ruled and how it is to be used so as to fulfil the purpose for which it was appointed, it is the burden of all His ministry. To see in Him the Father means to see that the world is ruled by a wise love working with His children for ends still too high for their knowing, but, through faith in which, they can meet life's trials with patience and have courage for its duties and discernment for its opportunities.

Therefore, it is either the greatest truth about the world ever set forth; or it is the greatest delusion ever cherished: and there can be nothing between.

But when theology divides into the rubrics of Theology proper, Anthropology and Cosmology, as matters apart, it separates God from His relation to the world and man, wherein alone we could know Him; and man from the rule that is over him and the right uses of the world about him, whereby alone he could be found to be more than the highest vertebrate animal; and the world from God's purpose in it and man called to realise this purpose, whereby alone there could be any possibility of seeing it to be a spiritual and not merely a material order.

The question before religion is precisely the relation of God to the world and man. Otherwise, God, man and the world become barren abstractions. Nor may we separate Jesus from the reconciliation of man to the rule of the Father amid all in the world that clouds our vision of it, and discuss in general the question of His nature, without reducing Him also to an abstraction. And the very reason for calling God's Spirit personal disappears the moment we separate Him from His work in the individual and the community, for, then, however loudly a personal Spirit is confessed, we have nothing but a mysterious potency.

Before, however, it would be worth while discussing such matters, we must first know where we stand on this question of whether the world is ruled by a Father in a love which is wise by seeing the end from the beginning wholly to be trusted, or by blind fate above and accidental happenings around to be met by a resolute will to endure and to withstand.

Should it, however, be that the true meaning of man is not what he is, but in what it is God's purpose that he should become, and the true meaning of the world not its evanescent changes, but the eternal good these changes are to serve, we could not discover this by any inference from man as he is, or the world as it is, or from both together.

That this is just man's greatest and most paralysing delusion is, at this moment, being vehemently affirmed. It is regarded as an opiate for the distress man himself ought to remedy and a distraction from the victories man himself ought to win.

As we have neither grasped the difficulty nor the decisiveness of faith in the rule of the Father, there is great gain in having it thus decisively denied. Regarded as a pious affirmation not to be doubted but also not to be regarded as of practical moment, it is even further from a genuine belief by which we may live than the most vehement denial, which at least realises its significance and may through sorrowful experience one day be brought to realise its reality.

How we ourselves stand in this matter we can know better by seeing it in a human life than by any discussion of it as abstract doctrine, and the life of Jesus alone should we think of considering.

In our critical days the difficulty might seem to be about the tradition of His life and teaching. But, while this also may not be evaded, very few people, in reading the Gospels, have much doubt that, in the main, one authentic voice speaks and one unique person is manifested. Nor is the difficulty about either the material or the mental ancient world in which Jesus lived. The real difficulty is the very modern question of the spiritual atmosphere. A vague impression that science has disposed of it is a hindrance to some: but the far greater hindrance is the assumption that the average opinions of our time are not the mere fashion of an age but enlightenment about eternal verity. When we expect God's blessing according to our self-esteem, His approval according to our self-sufficiency, and His aid according to our self-will, we cannot begin to see, for the Father's rule is according to His love and wisdom not our blindness and self-love.

The spirit of Jesus, the Apostle thought to be supremely manifested in His death, in which by bearing all the State could do of cruelty, the human heart devise of mockery of good, and religion show of formalism, hypocrisy, unscrupulousness and hard injustice, He enables us, as we are, to be friends with God, as He is, and trust His love in all, so that in everything we can give thanks. This challenges us in life and not merely in history.

His death, however, instead of manifesting God as always the Father of us all just as we are, amid events just as they are, is used to abstract from life except as what can die, from God except as a principle of justice and from ourselves except as provided with a device for evading our deserts.

But Christ's manifestation of the Father in death only crowns a life devoted in word and deed to the purpose of revealing His rule, which, as it deals with everything, can be tested by everything. Yet it is everything as God's love is the meaning and end of all, and, therefore, as He measures it and not as we do, except as we are of His mind: and even then only in dim hopes and aspirations, and not in confident application of the standards of value of our age or its notion of progress. What we esteem and our age values may be as great a hindrance to entering the world in which Jesus lived as what was esteemed and valued among His contemporaries. Even what passes as religion among us may be, in our time as in His, the greatest of all hindrances. To be ready to review the presuppositions of our age as well as our own preferences and prejudices, and not least in what we take to be our religion, is part at least of the child-like mind which alone can enter the kingdom.

As a general statement, the rule of the Father might be said to be—positively—pardon and succour according to need, and—negatively—not legal equivalent of award according to merit. But general statements are always inadequate and often misleading: and the very quality of our Lord's revelation of the Father is its relation to all experience. Hence it is not honestly dealt with till we realise that all our life and thought and action is at stake in the answer we give to it. It is a rule actual in all and over all, measured by eternity but manifest in time, with nothing beyond its orbit. Just through life's various aspects, Jesus shows the Father, not in abstract truth about Him, but in ways capable of being put to the test by experience as we find toward it the right attitude and shirk none of it.

1. Faith in the Father is the ground of our Lord's view of Nature

The uniformity of Nature is often taken to be the uniformity of indifference, behind which view lies the assumption that God should be a moral governor determining everything by exact material award according to merit and demerit. But to Jesus it is the uniformity of the wise goodness of a Father who sends His rain equally upon the just and the unjust, the evil and the good, and whose highest perfection it is to be kind to the unthankful and evil.

This is not difficult to accept, either as fine sentiment or as the hard idea that whatever happens is good for us, Nature having a very large family and no leisure to coddle them. But our Lord's view is far nearer the poet's seeing, in the silent face of Nature, unutterable love. And when it is granted us to look for moments into her face with something of the poet's eyes, who then sees merely the dead processes of the laboratory? But, while One who saw the lilies of the field clothed more gloriously than Solomon did not lack the poet's eye; for Him the way in which this faith can truly come home to us is by being perfect as our Father in Heaven is perfect, not in an austere and faultless morality, but in knowing no limit to the forgiveness of wrong, or prayer for those who despitefully use us and persecute us. When this is accepted, that the uniformity of Nature is a wise love can hardly be doubted. Anyhow, it is a matter of attitude not inference or argument.

2. It is the ground of our Lord's view of Human Nature

To begin with, there is this common relation of us all to Nature. If we are seated with an erring brother at our Father's table, may we regard it as the way of wisdom and goodness that he should have all the cuffs and we all the cakes? We should be very smug children indeed, if we always saw our outward state approve our inward virtue. Of this kind of self-approval we have quite enough even as it is. We need to be reminded, both when we see the sinner in high-handed prosperity and when sin has been paid its due wages in misery, whether spending his substance in riotous living or come to husks, not only that he is God's child but also that he is our brother. Those whom the religious leaders of His time lightly dismissed as lost, Jesus said He came to save; and of none did He despair. When even one is found there is joy in heaven; and, when beginning again his upward way with halting steps, his guardian angel is the greatest from God's immediate presence.

We may, however, also err on the side of sentimental softness as well as hardness. The evil doer is no more to be regarded merely as a pitiable case of weakness than as a hard case of obdurate wickedness. The parental idea often put in practice is that, every time the prodigal falls into the gutter, his father should be by to pick him up and his mother to brush his clothes. But the first thing the father of the prodigal recognises is his son's responsibility. When he wishes to go on his own, the father divides his living with him to make him really independent, and he goes. And the father does nothing till the son, by having to endure all the racket of his misdeeds, comes to himself, and so to the Father. To be mealymouthed about wrong may be mere condescension to a poor, weak, foolish creature, from whom you expect nothing better. "Thou shalt not hate thy brother in thy heart: thou shalt in any wise rebuke thy neighbour and not suffer sin upon him." But alas our rebuke is apt to be superior and not the human wisdom of a tried experience and the understanding love of an intimate fellowship. Hence it is more often met by resentment than by amendment.

Lately I read again John Woolman's *Journal*. The sins of the time lay heavy on his heart and the task of dealing with actual people about them was a weight upon his conscience. They were specially owners of slaves, oppressors of the Red Indians, and persons too set on prosperity for their soul's good. Not only alone, but generally also at the public service of worship, he first brought the matter before God. The result was, as he expresses it, that his heart was "tendered", a strange preparation we might think for such a stern task. The effect was to make him feel deeply the temptations of his brethren and the forces against which he too might have been weak. Then he went and said, in the most direct language he could command, what was given him to say: and, severe as it was, it was seldom resented. Few men ever did so much to redress wrongs as this plain man of no position and no conspicuous gifts, but with the supreme wisdom of dealing as brother with brother, which is the practical acknowledgement of one Father.

3. It is the ground of our Lord's view of Providence

In days of comfort, order, abundance and stability, Providence was affirmed as a self-evident truth of Natural Religion. But it could, in such circumstances, with equal ease be disregarded or even denied. Not in prosperous days, when it might seem not hard to believe in God's care, but, amid nations doomed and civilisation in decay, have faithful men been most assured that the Lord God omnipotent reigns. The most gracious view of it as the Rule of the Father was announced in an age vanishing amid the most overwhelming calamity, in which revolt, earthquake, famine and war were only the beginning of such tribulation as had not been from the beginning of the world. This Jesus saw, yet never doubted that we live in a world where the skill and care bestowed upon the grass of the field rebukes our anxieties about food and clothes, and that as even the sparrows share the Father's care, no kind of provision they need will be wanting to His children.

But while all things work together for good, it is only for those whose love responds to His, and whose call is according to His purpose, or in other words it is not for what we desire, but for what our Father's love and wisdom design for us. Nor can this be a merely selfish good apart from His whole purpose with all His children. Till we know not only our real good, but also the larger good in which we find it, we could not tell what works together for it. Yet again it is a matter of attitude and not of evidence: and if we have steadfastly set our hearts on the highest we can see, can we doubt that our Father's purpose is still higher, or that not accident but a wise goodness leads us forward?

4. It is the ground of our Lord's view of Prayer

Prayer being the children's intercourse with their Father, the assurance that God knows what we need before we ask Him and the sense that our asking makes it more God's gift and our good are in no conflict, but are God's most personal way of giving and ours of receiving. Yet in such personal intercourse there may be better answers than even giving and receiving, and therefore a better way of waiting upon God than besieging with repetition and insistence, because God may both have a better gift and a better way of giving. To help us to find by seeking may enrich us more than just to put it into our hands; and the highest of all may be what we can neither ask for nor seek because it is beyond our knowing. It lies behind blank doors at which we can only knock, yet which, if our whole life is a patient knocking at them, will open on discoveries we have not even imagined. Thus, as a father, God gives in the way that would make us most His children in freedom and power.

Here again the test is by attitude, not evidence, an attitude of earnestly desiring the best gifts, in which we are willing to be shown a more excellent way than either receiving or finding, because of a great expectancy respecting God's mind with us and for us.

5. It is the ground of His view of the Rule or Kingdom of God

What seems to be all contradiction when we set God and man over against one another, becomes the essential quality of the mind of the Father with His children when we keep them together. His rule is essentially moral and we are in it only as we have accepted it and live freely in it; yet we do not enter it according to how moral we are. It is catastrophic, yet its very quality is calm trust and inward peace which in the end works outward peace. It is wholly God's doing yet by a doing which is also man's. It is all of grace, but to be our graciousness. The present order is a contradiction of it; yet even in the present order it alone is invincible. Though for us to serve with all our strength and mind and heart, yet being God's rule not ours, it does away with all striving and crying.

What makes these complements seem contradictions is thinking of a potency not a father, for with a father and his children, that it is all of the father's wisdom and power does not make the child's part less important, seeing that what the wisdom and power seek most of all is the child's freedom, mastery and character. There is always unlimited good, yet it would only be good as it made us strong in the father's mind and likeness. It is waiting but only till it can truly bless. We do not need to strive, in anxiety and distress, for what is waiting to be given, even though it be only given as we receive and serve it. In short it is a rule of freedom ready to break in at any moment as a gift of God and yet which, being our freedom, must be of our willing, loyal and devoted allegiance.

This also approves itself only to the right attitude which is the expectation of great doings of God and patient acceptance of the discipline and duty by which He prepares us for it, with the recognition that, in a matter which concerns all that is at stake in us and for us, even great and overwhelming disasters may be blessed if the alternative is satisfaction with less than God's purpose, both for us and by us. If we are measuring life by less than God's end in it, we cannot, in short, hope to recognise God's rule over it.

6. It is the ground of our Lord's view of immortality

So far as He ever uses argument as a support for any belief it is for immortality, but it is purely on the ground of the need of the Father for his children. It is not merely that we cannot conceive that God's relation to us as our Father could end with the physical change we call death. A mere belief in another life is easy and may not be specially spiritual. The denial of it is not justified by any knowledge we have either of what is physical or mental; and the universal belief in it shows how naturally it springs from the human heart. But the confidence with which love affirms and ceases to be mere self-love is only justified in the Father's child who has set before himself the hope of attaining to the whole height of life in the family of God, in which he could be made worthy of immortality by the infinite vision, endless purpose, and measureless but exalting responsibility which could fill it. Our answer, therefore, depends on facing the high destiny of the children of God, not in theory but in the whole bearing of our lives: and if we live wholly in the temporal we cannot wonder if we have no sure faith in the eternal.

7. It is the ground of our Lord's view of pardon and grace

It is God's dealing with the sorrow and sin of the world that gives the essential quality to the meaning of God as Father; and it is the place of His lost children which marks the essential quality of His dealing with all His children. The supreme revelation of His mind is in seeking and saving the lost; and the end of all reasoning with Him is the discovery of a patient pardoning love which makes sin that may be as scarlet, white as snow. This restoration to our Father and His family alone gives reality to pardon, which otherwise is mere condonation. It is reconciliation to the Father's mind and restoration to His peace, with an assurance which can face our whole experience, however distressful it may be. Its test is that, in everything, we are enabled to give thanks and that from every failure we can rise in hope, and from every transgression return to peace. It is not even a question of the pure in heart seeing God, but of the impure seeing the Father, wherein the unique significance of the life and death of Jesus while we were yet sinners most appears.

CHAPTER IX

FAITH AND FREEDOM

IF this be the faith that saves, it could not be given either by an infallible Scripture or an infallible Church, even though backed by penalties in this world and the pains of hell in the world to come. Yet how much once deemed essentials of the faith seems to be crumbling from lacking them as foundation. Moreover, does not much more that remains depend on a traditional sentiment which originated with them and may still be parasitic on them, making many not question what is impressive and venerable? Is not faith still regarded by most of those who seem to swell the number of believers as what is imposed by authority? They still read the Bible as God's legislation not His counsel, and expect the Church to dictate in no uncertain tone what is to be thought and done, and would not know what they believe were this lost to them.

When this happens, and nothing else replaces it, the loss of help and guidance may be calamitous. If God's truth is able to witness to itself and God's children able to reserve it for themselves, it may be changing a temporal for an eternal foundation, but the danger and the delay encourage the demand to lay again the old foundation. When, however, it is thus the deliberate outcome of our fears, it is laying again a foundation of dead works, not of repentance from them. We need not go so far as infallibility either in Church or Scripture.

It is enough to regard the impressive more than the true and to venerate tradition more than present reality. We do not really believe except in freedom or prove except by what makes us more free. But this whole concern gives the impression that faith and freedom are opposites: and nothing so much turns the heart of honest people from religion.

There are however different ideas both of freedom and of faith, and, with that, of tradition. There are traditions which make void the living word of God and require slavish submission, and there are traditions which are as essential for freedom as for faith. Were our whole realm of freedom our own minds and its whole security our indomitable wills, it would be little to trust in. We need the kind of freedom which makes us indomitable. The root of all chaos is the disorder in our own minds, while trust in our own hearts is not merely one kind of foolishness, but is the sum and substance of all folly. Let us, by all means, rule the kingdom of our souls with courage and determination and have as indomitable souls as we know how. But to make this our boast, and not recognise it to be a humbling approximation at best, is rather a pitiable kind of pride. Unless we find, in the rule of God, liberty by the joy of the Lord being our strength, freedom is a mockery. What does freedom mean if the world is a series of mechanical happenings and our pain or pleasure in them the end, and that determined? Has even honesty any sense when the sole comfort is in illusion and there is nothing higher to make it wrong? But if we are the Father's children in our Father's world as our Lord taught about it and lived in it and died for it, and, however dimly we discern it, yet in our noblest and freest moments see in part that love is in all and over all and the end of all, then we are in some true sense free, and, the more we reach out to it, the more our honesty is emancipated from human hesitations, fears and compromises.

With respect to this faith, we are in the same position now as those who first went forth with it to the world as the good-news of God, having nothing whereby they could impose it except in freedom nor anything to commend it except the good-news in Christ of the liberty of God's children.

In the first place no humblest sect to-day is in a worse position for invoking the authority of the Church than those whose sole claim was, in Christ's stead, to be ministers of reconciliation. The Church which claimed the priestly succession and the divinely sanctioned organisation, not only repudiated their faith and works, but had condemned as a criminal the Master they preached. In their appeal to the Jews, therefore, Church authority was all against them; and in their appeal to the Gentiles it had no existence. Not only to the Apostle Paul himself, but for the whole purpose of his mission, even those who appeared to be pillars in the Christian Church itself were not of any account, and the attempt to impose their authority was to the Apostle a mere assault on the liberty wherewith Christ had set His people free.

In the second place, no criticism has left us in a worse position for any appeal to the authority of Scripture than the Early Church.

The Christian Scriptures were not yet written. Even the sayings of Jesus were only being repeated by those to whose hearts they spoke. No one had ever made such use of the Old Testament as Jesus, but He spoke with the direct authority of truth and not with authorities, not even the Scripture. As we have seen the Apostle Paul was even more startling in his freedom, though it was only a freedom wherewith Christ had set him free. In arguing with the Jews, he may seem to accept their literalism, yet only to meet dialectic with dialectic: and he is never so uninspired as when engaged in it. Not only did he reject the authority of the Law, which was to the Jew the most sacred part of Scripture, but to him none of it was commandment contained in ordinances, or to be read in any way that set limits to the freedom of him that is spiritual, in judging all things. Wherefore, the question, often asked to-day, of what is valid in Scripture if so much is called in question, has from him the answer that all of it is profitable for him who discerns truth because he loves God with all his mind, who knows right because he loves God with all his strength, and who gives a due value to others because he loves God with all his heart.

Nothing less is the final, Divine order, and nothing less is God's Kingdom or Rule, the possibility of entering which is the good-news of Jesus Christ. It is the freedom wherewith Christ sets us free, when no one need say, Know the Lord, for we see the Father; and no one need order our steps for the law of love written on the heart directs our ways. This is the only final order in the nature of things, and before we go further it is necessary to ask ourselves whether it is for us so great a good that the lower order of one person ruling another, however much it may be of temporary gain, can never be final without eternal loss.

This is the decisive question for our honesty, for the greatest trouble comes for most of us from trying to be Mr Facing-both-ways. We would all be free and have some respect for others' freedom, but we would be well guarded by the fortifications of authority and compulsion, not as mere temporary devices, but as something to be carried for safety though freedom should fall under its weight.

Only if the whole value for man's soul and his one way of entering the Kingdom is to receive it in the freedom of God's children, can we see meaning in the long weary road of error and sin by which God leads man. But, if we see this, we can also see that such times as ours, when forms, traditions, customs, organisations are being shaken may just be to show us what cannot be shaken if we have patience to abide the test, and that for our real victorious faith nothing may be so reinvigorating as the repudiation of what we have merely not taken the trouble to deny. Yet honesty requires us to sit down and count the cost and to realise that he who puts his hand to the plough and looks back is not fit for the Kingdom in which, in the nature of things, freedom and honesty know no reserves.

Yet if this is God's Kingdom, it is plain that we cannot realise its meaning and its purpose by ourselves alone. We are to be free in ourselves, but it is to find our freedom with all things and all men, and while we begin with being honest with ourselves, it is in order to be able to respond to all truth and be open to the claim of all righteousness and find therein our emancipation.

Truly honest freedom does not make us omniscient Ishmaelites, as many who pride themselves on possessing it in exalted degree seem to imagine, but is the only bond with others which can be loyal through all storm and stress. To the Apostle it meant being fellow-citizens with the·saints and of the household of God, which besides being the only perfect way of belonging to the only perfect fellowship, is also the only perfect way of possessing the heritage of the past, because to be built upon the foundation of the apostles and prophets, Christ Jesus Himself being the chief corner-stone, is to have a foundation which we prove, not as we are linked together by outward bonds, but as we each have access in one Spirit unto the Father, and thereby, as each finds his own place, yet is knit together in the service of the whole. Thereby we have both a Church and a revelation by which, and not merely in the face of which, we can maintain our freedom, because it is a fellowship of free response and a revelation of free persuasion. No one was ever freer in face of every possible situation than the apostles and prophets, except Jesus Christ Himself: and only thus can we build on them. But now comes the question of what this means for our honesty.

If, as has been maintained, it concerns either God's ultimate order or man's supreme delusion, and there is nothing between, it is not a matter for argument, or for correct opinion, or for edifying approbation, and to attempt to argue or bully or bribe us into accepting it is to deny our honesty and to hinder our freedom, and that for a kind of persuasion which would never make us more than conquerors.

As the good-news of God is specially through Jesus Christ, the question concerns Him above all; and to deal with it is the more necessary, that, at this moment, by nothing else is faith so much perplexed, and that though no other question is so insistent, the facing of no great question is so constantly evaded.

For shrinking from this task there may be bad reasons of timid orthodoxy, but there are also two good ones. The first is that no discussion by general consideration will ever do justice to what even we ourselves have found of His wisdom and power; and the second is that we cannot with modesty regard our own discernment as exhaustive of a love which even the Apostle says passes knowledge.

Yet modesty is committing ourselves to God's enlightenment for the answer, and never shirking great questions: and, considering the challenge of the present distress and perplexity, the enquiry may not with honesty be evaded.

When a very distinguished ecclesiastic spoke of it as a further triumph of faith, not only to believe in God, but also in Jesus Christ, a great many people would have thought it a very much greater and more difficult achievement, for instead of being the author and finisher of their faith in God, He has become an additional burden upon it.

Nothing could be in more amazing contrast to what Jesus signified for the good-news of God to its first ambassadors. With it they feared no enquiry however searching and no opposition however hostile. In His name, as never before, they worshipped the Father; in His service they rejoiced in freedom; in His Spirit they found a love in which they could triumph in all and over all. But, if now, instead of being the originator and finisher of a faith in the Father which triumphs over everything in time and change, were many honest with themselves He would be the first and greatest obstacle for faith to surmount, what, we must ask ourselves, has happened to cause so great a change?

Truth for us is what we know to be a right interpretation of experience when in perfect freedom we have allowed it to speak to us. Whether is the reason then that, if we thus deal with His witness, we do not discover the final order in which we live; or is it that we have sought His significance in other directions?

One is to seek it in experiences.

In their place they have doubtless helped to enlarge man's spiritual horizon: and possibly, some of us have unduly fought shy of them. Yet, what life should work of deepest assurance to the spirit is not so much experiences of comfort and hope as added confidence in Jesus Christ as interpreting all experience. Nor is there much about emotional experiences in Scripture or perhaps any sacred writing. To tell what God has done for one's soul is to speak of victories not of emotions. Moreover, though honesty of feeling is the first requirement for knowing truth, the proving of it is by application in thought and action. For a long time a singularly uniform experience of conversion under certain evangelical influences seemed evidence sufficient. But, when this no more came of itself and had to be stirred up, so far from being confirmation it gave a sense of unreality.

Another direction is to seek objectivity in an orthodox theology.

We cannot know the things of faith and love apart from what we ourselves actually believe and love, and, apart from human experience, build up truth from generalities. Few causes more than this have so hindered life from revealing to us its deepest meaning, for we learn only as we are humbly responsive to the highest we see and meet what it demands from us of loyalty and endurance. Though, if we live in the seen and temporal we do not live in the unseen and eternal, we can only find the unseen and eternal by the uses of the seen and temporal. Divorced from life, religious and anti-religious dogma alike are striving after wind. The question for us is whether, for directing us, amid the seen and temporal, towards the ends it should serve of the unseen and eternal, Jesus commends Himself as at once the truth which is guidance and the life which is strength. If we have experiences, their right place is not to stand by themselves but to be part of all experience.

From this we further stray by looking for something other than the mind of God in the face of Jesus Christ—a different mind, and a different order and a separate divinity.

This has mainly to do with what we have called questions of the lower honesty, chiefly historical and dogmatic, but, in our time, enormous interest has been devoted to them: and no honesty can ignore labour so extended and so devoted.

Yet it must be only in their due place; and due place is not first place. The time when certain views especially of the New Testament were regarded as a matter of life and death for religion has passed or should have. Nevertheless, the mere amount of writing on the subject still leaves the impression of supreme importance, and the piling up of one opinion upon another of a greater finality of result than facts justify.

But, while we have to keep such enquiries in their due place and due uncertainty, even about Jesus Christ there may be a wrong respect which is a dishonest consideration. Instead of anything being too sacred for discussion, the sublimer, more intimate, more vital for us it is, the more it demands devotion to every necessary enquiry.

Take, to begin with, the historical questions regarding the life and teaching of Jesus.

On the one hand, we may not dismiss as irrelevant the supreme interest for which the memory of them was cherished, which was His significance for man's relation to God. Nor can we separate anything He ever said or did from the kind of spiritual world in which He lived or even from our own belief in its reality or unreality. In comparison, even historically, the material situation is quite secondary. But, on the other hand, to assume the Christ, say of the Athanasian Creed, and seek to interpret the records thereby, is to make historical enquiry a mockery. An enquiry into the soundness of the foundations is not settled by pointing to the elaborate and stately edifice built on it. The more Jesus concerns our religious life, the more we are concerned to know what His own life and teaching were. For this we may not even assume that all the writers of the New Testament agree, or indeed that any of them mirror Him without distortion. Thus His view of Apocalyptic may be quite unlike *Revelation* and His view of His relation to God in no way as the Logos in John.

Here too the question arises whether history may not shade into myth, and our decision will largely depend on what we think possible for nature and human nature. Yet even myth may show a significance of religion for life and of life for religion which distinguishes it from superstition. More essential, practical truths may be found in stories fashioned in action and human relations, than in abstractions, even the profoundest ever produced by reflexion. Though this in no way justifies the easy settlement of the question of what is true in fact by saying it does not matter how much the turbid waters of phantasy are mixed with it so long as the whole reflects the face of the sky, we should not forget that there may be such a reflexion in them.

Yet few who read the Gospels with an open mind have much doubt about their historical and religious credibility on the whole; and the real difficulty begins for most with the expectation that they ought to read back into them the ecclesiastical formulations of dogma.

These were produced later to meet certain errors and explain certain difficulties; and they deserve to be considered for the end they served. But neither the method of abstract statement nor such matter as the substance of the Deity was from Him who spoke in parables for the express purpose of keeping faith in the Father amid life's actual requirements. Wherefore, they may not be appealed to in determining what a work of patience and labour of love can make out of the New Testament, and least of all of the life and teaching of Jesus.

CHAPTER X

JESUS AND THE KINGDOM

WHEN we speak of God, we mean the final and absolute power. Wherefore, if Jesus truly reveals the Father, He is a revelation of the rule of omnipotence, the love of God which He commends to us being nothing less than the absolute might. Sometimes it is said that God reveals Himself in grace and also in power. But grace is nothing if it is not the final power; and power is mere force if it is not grace. Wherefore, Jesus could say that all power was given Him of the Father: but it is in His own sense of all being for the rule of God as manifested by Him, and not in the sense of being Himself omnipotent. Though the fullness of the godhead which dwelt in Him in bodily form is a revelation of the nature and therefore of the true might of omnipotence, to turn what thus revealed the rule of love into mere might, and then transfer it to Jesus, is the same type of arguing from abstractions sent into the void as we have seen employed in other spheres. As in other spheres, it was a helpful, almost a necessary, simplification for a time. Especially in dealing with idolatry and the welter of evil spirits, it proclaimed in a way suited to the mind of the age that there is only one rule, which is merciful as well as mighty. But it had also the same mechanising effect, till now it is the chief reason why Jesus has become to many a stone of stumbling, instead of the chief corner-stone of faith in the Rule of the

Father. By reckoning greatness in terms of space, it seems to confine faith in Him to an age when the earth was the centre of the universe with mere vague infinity around, and tó be impossible for an age to which it is a sand-grain in one of half a million nebulae. But, while we think so much in space that material size is very difficult to keep out of our ideas of greatness, so then, though no one was ever freer than Jesus Himself from any wish to be so measured, upon no one else has it ever been so much imposed.

The most eloquent account of ascribing this kind of greatness to Him I know is Dryden's:

"What more could fright my faith than three in one?
Can I believe eternal God to lie
Disguised in mortal mould and infancy,
That the great Master of the world should die,
And, after that, trust my imperfect sense?"

But, unfortunately, this itself is just what frights the faith of so many, because it is the kind of faith which involves the material universe, and which, therefore, the vastness of the universe cannot but fright.

Nor is this the end of the trouble. An abstract omnipotence of like substance with the Father replaces the truth Jesus taught and the life He lived, which speaking through living human intercourse to men's own minds and lives, were the way to the Father. The divinity of Jesus, set forth by itself as a metaphysical principle and apart from the humanity it inspired and sustained and the love of the Father which appeals through it, reduces the humanity to an illusion and the divinity to an abstract symbol. A humanity which is a mere cloak for deity is not humanity at all; and, with a metaphysical deity as pure omnipotence, real religion has no concern. Faith has to do with God's mind, and only, through it, with His might, even though, if it be truly His mind, it has as much right to be regarded as significant of the quality of the universe as the understanding of motion for its quantity: and in the sense of being the supreme revelation of this mind in all and also the source of a new reconciliation to bring us into accord with it through all, Jesus has universal significance, or we might say significance for the universe.

His work to this end is set forth in the New Testament under three titles—the Christ, the Lord, the Son: and we can best deal with the question under these rubrics.

1. The Christ

The intimate connection of this title with the Kingdom or Rule of God is evident; because it means The Anointed, as its head and the embodiment of its power according to its real quality. Upon the nature of this Rule and how Jesus conceived Himself as the Messiah there have been endless learned disputations and the utmost differences of erudite opinion. Here it must suffice to take His own statement that to preach the Kingdom or Rule of God He had specially come forth. Therefore, what He conceived it to be must be much more completely evident in His whole teaching than in any particular quotation from it, and in His way of living and dying still plainer.

In a sense it was only the completion of what was taught by the prophets, which we have already considered as set forth by Hosea, as not by might nor by power but by God's Spirit. Its working is to make us sons of God in His freedom. This is summed up as grace, the effect of which was later described as righteousness and peace and joy in the Holy Ghost, and by Jesus Himself as finding such freedom and joy in doing God's will as is found in heaven. Its special quality is seen in the redeemed who are the redeeming. Though of this our Lord's sacrifice is the supreme and most efficacious example, it is not so by being singular and different from God's rule for any of us. Its quality is in being the fullest manifestation of what works by all the saints and is for the deliverance, through the Father's appeal in it, of all sinners. So far from being to appease God, it is the supreme appeal of what His love is and always will be. Therefore, all sacrifices ended with Jesus, because in Him we see the Father Who would have mercy and not sacrifice, and not because of any perfect satisfaction rendered to His justice. The Cross is supreme sacrifice, and all Christian life should, in its imperfect way, do what it does perfectly, which is to commend God's love over all the evils which seem to deny it. Had these not been so great, nothing so ghastly as the Cross would have been needed. But shame and agony and death and the scorn for seeming failure seem to deny God's love; and, as the Cross is all these, through them all it commends God's love, without limit in what He will do for our succour. Especially reconciling us to Himself, in face of all that alienates and while we are yet sinners, is to give us victory over the idea of God as occupied with rules, regulations and organisations, and with rewarding those who regard them with eternal bliss and those who contemn them with eternal woe. The idea of the Crucifixion then as a compensation to a God needing to be reconciled to us, is just a harking back to the religion of fear, which the commendation of God's love on the Cross was to cast out. Jesus represents a Father who acknowledges none as lost but who seeks and saves and in whose heaven there is joy over the humblest that is found. Restoration has no conditions whatsoever except just what God is and willingness to accept it. God invites us to come and let us reason together with Him to find His perfection to be, not mere stainless purity, but kindness to the unthankful and evil, in the sunshine of which, though our sins be as scarlet, they shall be white as snow.

2. The Lord

The way in which Jesus is Lord we may not separate from the way in which He is the Christ. Just as He reconciles us to God by commending His love to sinful men, in the midst of life as it meets us, and giving peace in its discipline and its duty as they are appointed us, so He would direct us therein that we should have victory and freedom. He objects to being called Lord, Lord, unless we do the things that He says, and unless we do them in His way.

The Apostle speaks of casting down every high thing —our own sophistries and all that exalts itself against the knowledge of God—and bringing every thought into captivity to the obedience of Christ. This probably means to the same kind of obedience to God as His, but, in any case, it is because of the nature of His obedience that He claims ours. This obedience Jesus Himself described as being meek and lowly in heart; and He meant the same when He said, Blessed are the poor in spirit, for theirs is the kingdom of heaven.

When poverty of spirit is assailed as slave-mentality the nature of the kingdom it gains is ignored. This is not being over-ridden even by God, and much less by man, but is the discovery of such a good and blessed rule that no place is left for resenting God's will or distrusting His help. Thus it is seeing in this appointment what gives us joy and in this requirement what gives us courage, so that it is both freedom with God and from man.

This so fills the horizon as to leave no room for compromise or mere deference to human opinion, but is the way in which, in peace and freedom, we can face all life requires of us as well as all it appoints for us, without hardness and without evasion. Nor, if to know God's mind is the only knowledge and to do His will the only right, is poverty of spirit before it different in essential attitude from the exclusive concern with reality whereby all progress in knowledge and discernment has ever been made. Jesus Himself, the most independent of all thinkers, the greatest of all innovators and the most calmly heroic of all conquerors, is surely sufficient refutation. Nor has He lacked followers who have found, just in His obedience, deliverance from custom, convenience and subjection to human opinions and human authority. So far from being weak submission, this poverty is the call to seek safety by ceasing to hug the shores of convention, custom and hesitating prudence, and going out to the open sea with no guidance except the lights of heaven.

3. The Son

Jesus manifests the Father by being perfectly the Son, not by being Himself the Father. It is as the Son that He is both Christ and Lord, and reconciliation thereby is to make us sons of God, the whole difference in the service being that it is done in the freedom of children and not as the servitude of slaves. The call which came to Him at His baptism as God's beloved son in whom He is well pleased dominated all His ministry. In nothing else, it is plain, did Jesus feel Himself so unique, yet, also in nothing else was He so closely identified with all His brethren, His very uniqueness being His significance for enabling men to become sons of God. Even when we say that He had it in Himself and we only through Him, it is not a different sonship except in originality and effect from what we all ought to have. His sonship, as has been said, is neither physical nor metaphysical, but is a relation to God through which He was sure of showing the heart of the Father and of all things being given Him of the Father that He needed. Yet even this is not a wholly unique position in our Father's house, for, when we are sons, we also see the Father, and, when we have the mind of Christ, all things are ours.

His true significance as the Son is summed up in the Apostolic benediction—The grace of our Lord Jesus Christ which unites the love of God and the fellowship of the Holy Spirit.

It has been said that Jesus was so great that His followers broke up the idea of God to put Him in. But the reason why He had followers at all was that their idea of God was broken and He brought it into one. Even the prophets had left unreconciled the bitter contrast between what they experienced in their own lives and saw in the lives of the godly and what they felt of God's mind and purpose in their own higher aspirations and their most spiritual fellowship. And for how many still is the great unsolved enigma why God's outward dealings should conflict so bitterly with His inward promptings. But the grace of our Lord Jesus Christ, by victory over the darkest, saddest, most conflicting experiences through which men can pass, sets them in the light of God's infinite purpose of love and provides for us a spiritual fellowship, both Divine and human. Thereby it shows the world of our outward and our inward experience to be alike from God and for ends for which in everything we may give thanks. Therefore, if man's world is to be renounced, it is that God's world should be possessed, which alone is the full recognition of one God in all and over all, of which mere abstract oneness of the Deity is not even the shadow. Thus the Apostolic blessing is not a metaphysical doctrine of the Godhead, but is a summing up of the whole Christian faith in redemption by reconciliation with the God whose love directs all and whose Spirit by fellowship inspires all.

Yet granting that the grace of our Lord Jesus Christ thus unites the love of the Father over all with the fellowship of the Spirit as inspiration and guidance through all, and so makes God one for us in the unity of all experience without and within, does this not, you may ask, still go beyond honest recognition of the limits of our knowledge?

And knowledge in the strict sense it is not. It is still mystery, in the proper meaning of mystery, as that which beckons us onward to know more by following what we see. It is a mystery of godliness, a mountain of God that rises on our vision as we fare forward climbing upwards, not a cloud in the skies of Church authority.

CHAPTER XI

FURTHER QUESTIONS

BUT granting that this is in Scripture, is there not much else besides that speaks to different purpose: and, if it do not speak to us, what then?

How much difficulty this presents depends on what we take the revelation in Scripture to be. If it be God's proclamation for His subjects, the more it is out of accord with our minds, the greater the homage in deferring it. But if it is counsel for His children, we may not attempt to impose it on ourselves, counsel being taken only when it persuades and becomes our own.

For many, however, the very idea of revelation is the imposition of information and injunction. Then some accept it implicitly for what they take to be the faith, and others reject it utterly for what they take to be freedom. But have we faith except won in freedom, or freedom unless maintained by faith?

Suppose, you say, we take a crucial instance. Paul is regarded, perhaps to-day more than ever, as the final interpreter of Christianity. But, in his interpretation, do we not find a Christ who appeases God's wrath; rules a special kind of kingdom; is the medium of creation as of reconciliation? Now supposing we reached the conclusion that this is so without dubiety, and, with equal certainty, that it neither persuades us nor helps us, what are we to do?

The answer is that we have only to take the Apostle at his word and follow his example. His word is that only by manifestation of the truth does he commend himself to every man's conscience in the sight of God. Then if with all openness of truth and right, before God and without personal or party consideration, we are not persuaded, we are to follow his example and take the same liberty with him as he very freely did with Moses.

Yet, when freedom with the Apostle is won, there may be less to reject than we think. As the full discussion of this would involve questions of interpretation too extended to be entered on here, I can only give my own general impression.

The Christ is for the Apostle one who is for the manifestation and realisation of God's Rule. His is a kingdom He hands over to the Father that He may be all in all. There is only one passage which seems to suggest that God needs to be reconciled (Rom. iii. 21-26), and one that Christ is creator as well as reconciler (Col. i. 16, 17). Now considering how these ideas dominated once they were received, the latter with the early fathers and the former with the Evangelicals, that they should be flung out in two isolated statements is surely incredible, especially as the Apostle's conviction about God sparing nothing to reconcile men to Himself and the spiritual significance of the grace of our Lord Jesus Christ are continually emphasised. Nor has he the idea of law which would need sacrifices to meet its claims; nor of efficacious rites which need a concentrated potency of Deity. The humanity of Jesus was as real for him as for Mark. On the physical side Jesus was of the seed of David, and shared the likeness of sinful man under the law; on the spiritual, he was God's Son by a spirit of holiness, and was exalted by way of loyalty, most conspicuously manifested on the Cross. Though undergoing the stern discipline which sin brings on His brethren, He Himself knew no sin. Yet it was only because He knew no separation from the Father, not because He could know no temptation. To express this significance the Apostle calls Him the Son of God, the likeness of God, the fullness of God, a life-giving spirit, the heavenly Christ, the heavenly man, the second Adam. But the explanation of them all is that God made man in His own image, and Philo calls the ideal man the Image of God, the Son of God, the Word of God. This perfect human reflexion of God is secured by a special relation, yet is what we should all have through Him who is the revelation of God's mind, showing His purpose in all things. Wherefore, however unique in perfection, the sonship continues to be a moral manifestation in the development of a true human life, and so remains within the things of the spirit.

Therefore, the real meaning of the passage in Romans must surely be that the kind of propitiation which is in Christ is to show not only that God is righteous, which we all acknowledge, but that He brings into a right relation with Him the ungodly, which we greatly need to learn. Then, considering how isolated the Colossian passage is, it is probably an interpolation to meet a later form of heresy.

But are there not passages, if not in Paul's writing, then in the Prologue of John and in parts of Hebrews, which make the Christ not merely the end of creation as the fullest revelation of God's purpose but the means of it? And what about them?

Possibly these writers expected more deference than Paul. But, if so, it was from being further from the source, in which case their right to it would be less. Yet, with them also, when we win freedom and are no more afraid of being over-ridden by merely imposed ortho-doxy, what they say may appear less incredible.

When we forget how much, to the ancient mind, the ideal was a sort of material reality, yet was not material, we take it to mean more than was intended. The Logos, Athanasius says, was at once in the bosom of the Father, ruling the world, and in Jesus Christ. Obviously he has no idea of a Divine which is absent from heaven when present on earth: and some in our day have found in this Logos an interpretation of science as well as faith. But, if it seem to you a materialising for materially-minded people, a useful simplification in face of fears of demonic powers and gods many and lords many, though honesty requires you to treat it with reverence, it also requires you not to carry it as a mere load upon your freedom.

But, you ask, what about the title Son of Man? Is it not of frequent use by Jesus Himself; and is it not in relation to a Rule or Kingdom of God conceived much more catastrophically and materially?

Here again I can only state my own impression, which is that the Son of Man is always used by Jesus for His cause and never, apart from it, of Himself. The source of the name is Daniel vii. 13–18, where it means the saints of the Most High who are to rule in peace and righteousness. This derives from the servant of the Lord in Second Isaiah; and it again from the Holy Remnant in First Isaiah; and it again probably goes back to the

7000 who had not bowed the knee to Baal. As no one ever interpreted the Old Testament more spiritually than Jesus, He could hardly have failed to realise that this remnant was to be a light to lighten the Gentiles and the glory of God's people Israel: and it is very improbable that He conceived this more materially. What apparently He did think was that He had come just for the realisation of its mission to seek and save, and this in its own way of victory by sacrifice and service and giving life as a ransom. At first He includes in this all His followers, but as the task narrowed down to His own manifestation and His own sacrifice, its death and victory are embodied in Him alone. Yet it is its fate not His own which is emphasised by the use of the title Son of Man.

Interest in the life of Jesus followed interest in what He signified for faith. Wherefore, the Epistles came first and the Gospels later, so that, the first thing we know about Him is that He gave a faith in the love of God which transformed lives and transfigured hearts. This cannot be set aside even if the Gospels indisputably showed either a calmly rational teacher or a fanatic under contemporary obsessions, because, for one thing, this is earlier than any gospel.

One of the conditions of our humanity is to have to meet life with the intellectual and even the spiritual limitations of our time: and Jesus would not have lived a truly human life on other conditions. Wherefore, we may not, on any general principle, decide what ideas of His contemporaries Jesus shared. Yet we may not affirm any more than deny merely on a general principle. One commonly applied is that, the cruder the idea, the nearer to the original source. But both history and experience seem to show that it is the original mind which sees with intellectual and spiritual freedom and the less favourably endowed followers who materialise and formalise. And surely Jesus would of all men be an unlikely exception. Nor if we do not force phrases, but take His general teaching and bearing and how they were received and understood, can there be much dubiety that His followers did not idealise them.

Nevertheless, the Kingdom with Jesus is decisive, and may be catastrophic, and therefore much nearer Apocalyptic than progressive moralisation of mankind. We are not less or more in the Rule of God, but are either for what Paul afterwards calls the Anarchy of Darkness or for the Rule of the Son of God's love. People are divided into saints and sinners, not by their virtues, but by their loyalties: and seeing that when loyalty to His Kingdom is won, the Father can and will do all things, we may look in hope, not for the slow process of education, but for a great transformation of all things by a faith which gives new aims, new succour, new peace. This is just as apocalyptic as the prodigal starving in rags in a far country one day and being at home clothed in splendour and feasting in magnificence the next. The way of living now in His Kingdom is to pray for the true worship, the true rule, the true consecration, the true use of material things by subordination to the spiritual, forgiveness realised in mercy and peace as we exercise the forgiving spirit of our Father among our fellows and meeting trial and temptation by having, like our Master, nothing in us to which the Prince of this world might appeal.

As this is the Rule of God, the way of bringing it to full fruition must be like it. Great disasters have their place, but it is only to teach the folly of the world-rule that men may see the vanity of their trust. This is a day of the Son of Man because it may be a day of the Kingdom.

And this is linked up with our heritage of evil, into which we enter as surely as into the heritage of good, with far-reaching determination of what we are to inherit.

Next as to the Flesh.

This is specially supposed to be derived from the Apostle Paul. But while the flesh is the sphere in which the sinful principle shows itself, it is not for him the sinful principle itself.

Neither spirit nor flesh is part of his division of human nature. Man is mind in substance and body in form. But he lives in contact with two worlds—spirit and flesh: and he may be drawn up mind and body into the eternal—the spiritual; or sink mind and body into the corruptible—the fleshly. Yet, while they that are in the flesh, in the sense of succumbing to the control of carnal appetite and desire, cannot please God, the sinfulness is the failure of the spirit to maintain its sovereign seat, not the usurpation of the flesh.

This view of the place of the flesh is not really different from the evolutionary view of the relation of evil to our animal heritage. If we develop conscience and fall back from conscience to impulse, is it not the sinful state of turning back on the upward road, of seeing and approving the better and following the worse, which is not merely a sinful act, but a sinful state?

In the Old Testament we find a long development of the idea of sin. Though never without a sense of being against God, it was first felt most strongly as disregard to tribal custom, then as breaches of statutory law, finally, with the prophets, as more of the nature of idolatry of the heart.

From this last the New Testament conception starts. Transgression is still conscious breach of law, and, as God's world will only serve His purpose, the way of transgressors is hard, and, in this sense, under the wrath of God. This is sin, but is not all sin, and all are not sinners in this way. Jesus loved the young ruler who had kept all the commandments from his youth; and Paul could claim to be, as touching the law, blameless. Especially in the Gospels negative breaches of the law, however gross, are made less of than lack of positive consecration of heart and life. Hence sin is a wider conception than transgression, embracing all lack of earnestness and sincerity in seeking to know God's purpose as well as in fulfilling what we do know. Just because God is God, all short-coming must be sorrow as well as loss. Hence all disloyalty to the highest we see and all lack of devotion to seeing it is sin. And, if so, have we not all sinned and come short of the glory of God, even though it may have to do with what we never reached rather than a state we lost?

But, granting this, what, to the end of victory over it, is meant by sin being forgiven? How does it alter anything that has been done?

> "Nor all thy piety nor wit
> Shall lure it back to cancel half a line,
> Nor all thy tears blot out a word of it",

is surely even truer of our actions than of our fate.

Guilt can be overlooked, but that is merely condoning, not removing or even meeting the consequences. For ourselves, sin blunts the insight, weakens the will, creates enslaving habits. How is this affected by forgive-

But here you ask, are we not forthwith weltering in a bog of unrealities?

First of all, is it the object of faith that saves? Then, we have what is called the Catholic Faith, which if anyone would be saved he must believe every detail of, the whole being a long series of what are only intellectual puzzles and not even mysteries. But, if genuine belief is what holds us, not what we resolve to hold, how can we really believe what has for us no concrete meaning? At best it could be only not denying, which, in such matters, is neither faith nor honesty.

If, however, it be faith as a state of our minds that matters, is that more honestly or more truly faith which the modern Evangelist evokes by playing upon emotion to over-ride reflexion, usually with forms which are only meant to be impressive, not to have any particular meaning?

Does either one or other give us any good reason for believing except, however it be concealed, the threat of hell and the bribe of heaven? surely, for such a reason, deliberately to attempt to twist our minds in certain directions is the very essence of dishonesty!

Yet, you further ask, is it better, if we return to the Apostle and ask what he offered for belief? The gospel which he said he had received, doubtless meaning thereby what was current in the Church when he entered it, and which he himself put in the forefront of his own message, was that Jesus Christ died for our sins according to the Scriptures. To many this has been the heart of the gospel ever since, being understood as transferring our guilt to the innocent. Now can we honestly believe that God would be satisfied with anything so unreal and perverted; or could we with any honesty avail ourselves of it if He were?

But was this the meaning of the original good-news, and is it because of this theory, or in spite of it, that it has seemed to be good-news to many since?

Every personal relation, if presented in theory, is necessarily misrepresented, and theories of the atonement are the worst misrepresentations. In a sense all friendship, which bears obloquy and suffers loss on another's account, is substitution. But a substitutionary theory, however it be dressed up, is sophistry, and unattractive sophistry, which is not improved by being attached to what is called the mystical unity. Also in a sense friendship bears the payment of sins not one's own. But the Penal Theory is a mere gross travesty of this, being legal juggling of the most repellent kind.

Is this, however, the true meaning? "According to the Scriptures" must be specially in accord with the suffering servant in Isaiah. There, however, the idea that it is of God that he is afflicted is a grave misunderstanding. Nor is there any suggestion that God derives satisfaction from this treatment of His servant. The suffering is at once from human wickedness and victory over it by the way the suffering is borne. In this sense the chastisement of our peace was upon Him and with His stripes we are healed: but it is a sense hid from the wise and understanding and revealed to babes, because an intellectual statement is more or less a legal formulation, and the essential revelation is that such is not God's way.

This accords with what Jesus Himself said after being recognised as the Christ. It belongs, He says, to the very nature of the rule of the people of God to be God's supreme appeal to His sinful children by suffering, without hardness and without evasion, the oppression of their evil ways, and the Christ is to be in the forefront of this way of seeking victory. The perfection of the Father is to be kind to the unthankful and evil, and the perfection of His servant to show this mind in all circumstances whatsoever.

That Christ died on account of our sins means first that they brought Him to His death. An important aspect of this is that it came by avoiding no task His help to sinful men required and what human hypocrisy, legalised cruelty and mass-hatred imposed. Doubtless it also means that He thus suffered through our sins to be a succour from them, yet it is as a way of dealing with the actual situation according to God's mind of pardon, pity and succour, and in no way to change His mind. Therefore, the object of faith is the love of God in all, and over all, forbearing with all evil that springs from man's freedom, yet never defeated by it. This is through Christ, who commends God's love in dying while we are yet sinners: just because of the many ghastly evils in life in face of which God's love has to be commended, the Cross was needed, but, then, there should be nothing we also may not meet, as Jesus did, without hardness and without evasion.

This new principle then is that the order of legality has become the order of love, and we have it by faith, not as mere intellectual conviction but as the effect of an order when we live in it, being the kind of knowledge upon which we cannot but act. As we have faith in the visible world by being in it, so we have faith in the spiritual. Though not an action but an ultimate reverence of the heart, action necessarily follows as we walk by the things unseen and eternal. This is described as being in Christ, which means not a mere mystical idea of almost physical union, but being in the Rule of God as the spiritual world with all its opportunities and succour.

Full deliverance would only be when we are free from both the attraction and the menace of sin by everything in us being changed. We are, therefore, only being saved. Yet, though in no other way, we possess its security in hope, the ground thereof being a change of relation to God, which itself is in a very real and effective sense, the forgiveness of sin.

Above all it is being enabled to forget the things that are behind and, unhampered, to press on to what is before. Chiefly this is by being finished with the idea of sin as breaches of law, what the Apostle calls the law of commandments contained in ordinances. This, he says, Christ abolished, nailing it to His Cross, meaning thereby that Christ put an end to this whole way of looking at life, by revealing a God determined not by rules of equity but by a pardon and succour that never wearies and never withholds and never spares itself.

In one sense the faith which saves into this love may be even more sensitive to the sin of the past and more ready to bear the blame and suffer the consequences. But it is as a present duty, to be done in the light of God's pity and encouragement with us and the transforming power of good before us, and no more as the overshadowing of a dark cloud of condemnation behind.

CHAPTER XIII

POWER TO FORGIVE SINS

THE affirmations of the sinlessness of Jesus in the Gospels are mainly in John. They are specially two. The first is "Which of you convinceth me of sin?" (viii. 46); and the second "The prince of this world cometh, and hath nothing in me" (xiv. 30). Like much else in this gospel, they may be reflexions on what Jesus was found to be rather than exact reproductions of His words. On such a matter, a claim made for Him is a greater testimony than a claim made by Him: yet if it be merely the denial of all conceivable defect, it would be a universal negative which no testimony can cover. In substance, however, both are positive assertions which can be subjected to positive tests.

The first has to do with seeing and serving the truth, and asks, who can say that Jesus ever came short in either?

Sin, being both self-deception and self-surrender, always leaves some blindness to truth and weakening of loyalty to it. But is there anything so certain and so amazing as the clearness of insight and unswerving devotion of Jesus, which shows no trace of His ever having suffered from obliquity of vision or moral evasion?

The second has to do with facing the end: and what it says is that, come what may, it will find in Jesus no wrong desire to bribe or weakness of fear to dismay.

Here too is a way of standing secure, which has nowhere else even a vague parallel. There is no callousness, no hardness, no mere austerity, but love of all truly good things in life, especially of all human friendship, which is sensitive, responsive, capable especially of spiritual suffering. Yet, when it came to losing all good and suffering all ill, there is nothing in Him that desires anything or fears anything against the will of the Father. This will He sees by giving to it all His mind, and the love in it He feels by giving to it all His heart, and the goodness of it by serving it with all His strength.

With nothing less could we stand finally secure in the Rule of God; and it is into this that we are being saved. And in face of all that our failures mean of blindness, weakness and openness to assault of wrong, can we doubt the need of some kind of dealing with our sin which may enable us to live in a new world with new peace and hope, and to look forward with sensitive and sincere souls to what is before, without being shadowed by what is behind?

Granting this, however, when we rid ourselves of traditional phraseology, what vital import for the situation can we attach to the forgiveness of sins? Even if only as condonation, forgiveness, as deliverance from such an external consequence as hell-fire, had a meaning. But, if the consequences are spiritual and in the sins themselves and manifest in blinding custom and paralysing habit and harking back and exposure to unworthy motives, and are not confined to ourselves but of evil influence and evil effect for others as well, what does forgiveness of sins do that it should be put in the forefront of all spiritual blessings and all transforming experiences? With the Jews, we could agree that God alone can forgive sin, but, if it mean the right to forgive ourselves in honesty before our own consciences and to be finished with them in justice to others, can even God forgive?

Nor, when we conceive it merely negatively as a blotting out of the past and merely abstractly as a transaction of omnipotence in the heavens, have we any answer to this question.

No one was ever so sure as Jesus of the Father's unlimited and unconditional forgiveness, with no one excluded unless by hypocrisy he shut his mind to God's mercy. Yet the faith which knows God's forgiveness to be real and transforming rests on Jesus because He lived and died setting this forgiveness in the heart of human experience and not merely proclaiming it.

He incurred the obloquy of eating with publicans and sinners as His genuine friends, not to condone their sins, but, by showing His regard for them in spite of what they had done and His readiness to face with them the shame of it all, to introduce them to the mercy and love of God which would do the same. All His dealings with those whom His righteous contemporaries regarded as lost were of the same order as the best robes and the fatted calf with which the prodigal was welcomed home, not something over and above forgiveness but witnesses to the restoration to the father's home and the father's heart, which is the significance of forgiveness. His whole life as well as His death was a commending of this love to sinners: and forgiveness is being saved into this love.

Even His work, however, is not to stand alone. He

healed the paralytic to show that the Son of Man had power on earth to forgive sins. As we have interpreted this name, it means the saints of the Most High. To them He says power is given to forgive sins, and the saying that what the disciples loose on earth shall be loosed in heaven is to the same effect.

But here you feel that honesty has a duty to put in a caveat. Consider all the claims to authority to forgive sins that have been based on this promise. There may be no objection, in view of a God who is kind to the unthankful and evil, that He has committed to His ministers to declare to all who are penitent and unfeignedly believe His holy gospel the forgiveness and remission of sins, and any of us may be His minister for this purpose to anyone. But what does it amount to? Even with remission, our honesty may have difficulty, but forgiveness in the deep sense is not done by declaring, even if on God's behalf.

What then of the idea of Aquinas that the pope's writ runs in heaven as the emperor's on earth? Apart from its failure to commend itself to our honest conviction, and the moral abuses of it when interpreted by indulgences, in what transforming sense could it be called forgiveness? Have not all kinds of conditions been tacked on to it, which show that, in itself, it is a mere legal transaction of remitting consequences, but leaving the sin still to be dealt with, and that largely by ourselves?

But what Jesus says is power, not authority: and that is to make forgiveness of such efficacy for inward peace and outward strength as His healing was to the paralytic. To have this power is to be enabled to show a friendship not turned aside by any degeneracy, and a fellowship ready to share the shame and misery of any iniquity: and the saints of the Most High are, above all, those who have the perfection of the Father in His kindness to the unthankful and evil and whose whole world is determined by a love which surrounds all in pardon, pity and succour.

The positive efficacy of forgiveness is in being born again, out of our world of resentments and bitterness and vengeance and weighing of awards, into this world of the rule of God's love and the fellowship of His Spirit. It is not merely leaving the house empty, swept and garnished, out of which the lusts of the flesh have been driven for the seven devils of spiritual pride to enter, but it is the positive introduction into the kingdom and its fellowship which gives at once humility in view of their infinite reach and confidence in view of their unlimited succour, just through the human love which knows how to make pardon a transforming reality.

But, wait, you say. Is not this a little too eloquent for our pedestrian honesty to follow? Apparently "The Son of Man" is very much what afterwards came to be called the rule of the saints. But is not the very quality of their rule, and for that matter of all who pass as saints whom you ever came across, that their whole attitude to life is constant disapproval? Do they not spiritually as well as materially think that, because they are virtuous, there will be no more cakes and ale? Have there not been various attempts at their rule; and, however these might differ, has not the hall-mark of all been repression? You may admit that, in spite of all God's love, just because He is God, there can be nothing good alien from

His purpose, and very great disaster in seeking to use His world for other ends, and that, in consequence, there may be a sharp crisis between being in God's rule and being out of it, but is all this harsh concern with the wrong, the way of commending the right? Burning you at the stake—which itself takes a belief in the rule of the saints to justify—is hardly the way of commending the Father's love to us while we are yet sinners; and is it better if the burning be deferred to the world to come? Can we say that any rule of the saints has ever done much to show that they were able to forgive sins by lifting us up by human lovingkindness into the love of the Father?

Perhaps also of individual saints your experience may have been unfortunate. Their way of being concerned either with their own souls or with yours has not given you much sense of a love and pity which could lift up your weary, burdened and sinful spirit to the love and pity of God.

But as nothing is so bad as bad religion, just because religion is the most vital of all realities, so nothing in it may be more oppressive than a rule of the saints which is the perversion of God's real rule. Let us remind ourselves again that the chief cause of the Crucifixion was what regarded itself as a rule of the saints, and also that the Cross is a victory over this kind of rule above all.

The true rule of the saints is by the Fellowship of the Spirit, and into it there is no entrance except in the liberty of the children of God by insight and consecration. For it none of these outward forms have any significance; and to it every method of compulsion is contrary. Forgiveness is both significant and secure only in the right sphere of its operation, which is the Fellow-ship of the Spirit. This is manifest among us in the fellowship of those who, by unlimited human pardon, pity and succour, have power on earth to make the forgiveness of God a transforming reality. Thus the graciousness of our Lord Jesus Christ unites the love of the Father with the fellowship of the Spirit, in the assurance that even the worst without and the highest within may be one in meaning and purpose.

But here it may again be felt that honesty has to call a halt. What is meant by the Spirit? As commonly understood, is it not a vague potency, operative for some through material rites and for others through mass emotion? Possibly more spiritual influences may be felt through both, and perhaps there are people who need these rather material embodiments, and we may all have need of some material forms for even our most spiritual perceptions, yet, for you, this seems too like savage ecstasy and the concentrated mysterious potency of savage magic to be a way to which you could honestly return, even granting it to have been a necessary stage through which mankind had to pass. Forms which to us are retrograde we may not observe without the grave sin of facing backwards, yet we must be sure that in thinking them retrograde we are not merely vaunting the old confident honesty which is impressed only by what can-not be ignored. Even if the forms be outworn, the truth they embodied may not. Nor may we limit this to what is plain to our understanding. Much that we believe most surely and find of the greatest practical significance is quite beyond our explaining, so if we have experiences of practical moment, we may not dismiss them because they are unique and cannot therefore be demonstrated by anything else. Yet, if we feel among even the most imposing forms like Ruth amid the alien corn, we are not to force ourselves into thinking them the native home of our spirits. Nay, if they are our own, and instead of helping to light up the whole landscape of nature and human nature are the sort of lightning flashes which shut it all off in darkness, it is time we tried the spirits, whether they be of God.

CHAPTER XIV

REVELATION TO BABES

To commend God's love is to do more than assure us of an amiable sentiment towards us in the heavens. The love of Him, from whom and unto whom are all things, also assures that all things work together for good to all who, in His way, seek what, in His sight, is the good.

For yourself, however, you have never had any reason to suppose that your own life was divinely guided for your particular benefit as if it were the favoured object of God's care. Nor are you sure that you desire it. Better perhaps bear the ills we have than live in the chaos· which would arise were everyone's idiosyncrasies individually considered. Nor when, with sensitive and sympathetic heart you look around, could you desire such favouritism so ill shared, and often least by the noblest and best. Does not the very Apostle who speaks most confidently on this matter also say that the stewards of God's mysteries are the off-scourings of all things until now and of all men most miserable if they have hope only in this life? Does not, then, his experience contradict his theory, for surely there cannot be much of all things working for good in this life if it is so unsatisfactory that another life has to be called in to redress the balance?

Yet the explanation is simple enough. It is in this life that all things work together for good, but not as if this life were all. The stewards of God's mysteries would of all men be most miserable were this life all, because they would be of all men most deluded, seeing that though the mystery has to do with this life, it is this life set in a larger. It is not that they have a wretched existence only to be sustained by hope of compensation, but that they would no more see life's real working without the power of an endless life. All things work together for good in this life, but not for what is confined to it. Nor is it necessarily for our own individual life, here or hereafter. We are in God's family where the general good is the good of each and there can be joy in serving it even with personal loss and sacrifice; we are not in God's hospital where we have private nursing, special doses and individual regimen.

In the nature of things, however, such a system can be good only for those who live in the spirit of it, which is spoken of by the Apostle as those who love God and are called according to His purpose. Nor, if God is God and this is His world, could we expect it on any other condition.

But two difficulties at once beset us: and they are difficulties in which our honesty as well as our understanding are involved.

The first is about loving God. Which of us can say that we love God with all our mind and heart and strength, and prove the reality thereof by loving our neighbour as ourselves? Moreover, does not all gush about loving God give a painful sense of unreality in the working up of sensuous emotion?

The second is about God's purpose. If it be beyond all we ever saw or heard of or could imagine, how can we be called according to it?

No doubt a man's reach should exceed his grasp, and toward the distant mark we best run our race. But, on the other hand, is there any greater humbug or more dishonest dealing with life's common relationships and immediate tasks than floating above earth's common tasks and trials on the wings of phantasy? How then can we conceive the unreality of what is beyond even our conceiving? Should we not need to be what the Apostle calls stewards of the mysteries of God? But who is bold enough or brazen enough to assume that role?

Yet the Apostle himself seemed to think it the ordinary state of the ordinary believer. The reason is that to him the mysteries are concerned with life not theory, not recondite matters of the intellect but the dimly felt call of the heart, which is known as, in stewardship for responsibility and service, we follow on to know. So conceived, it is not confined to religion, but the religion of Jesus Christ is the conscious acceptance of the call which has led man in his progress from the beginning.

In the New Testament the word translated mystery is of fairly frequent occurrence. It is the knowing in part which is a challenge to follow on to know, the following being, not by reflecting or reasoning, but by marching forward in the path along which it beckons. It is thus moral as well as spiritual, the seeing further being dependent on taking the step already seen. It is called the mystery of the Kingdom of God or simply the mystery of God, of that rule so far beyond our knowing, yet our call, our inspiration, our direction and the crown of all our endeavour.

This is what Jesus thinks is hidden from the wise and understanding and revealed to babes. Both in Matthew and Luke this is connected with "All things are delivered me of my Father", and knowledge of the Father through Him. But in Matthew there follows, apparently as part of it, the invitation to come to Him who is meek and lowly in heart and find rest for our souls: and doubtful as Matthew's connections often are, the relation of such apparent opposites is far more like Jesus than Matthew. The revelation is hidden from the wise and understanding and revealed to babes; it is a way of carrying our burdens by learning of Christ to be meek and lowly in heart; and, while these burdens include the intellectual and spiritual as well as the material, it is not by way of intellectual superiority or spiritual selectness.

But can we imagine anything more repugnant to our age than subordination of understanding and wisdom? Has not understanding to do with knowledge of the past, and wisdom with applying its lessons to the present? Did we not explain everything by the past and not by any purpose for the future? An age dominated by the idea of evolution cherished the comfortable optimism of assured and even progress: yet no age ever more looked backward for guidance or regarded any explanation by future purpose as so entirely unscientific. To trace the history and have a theory of the origin was the one idea of understanding anything; and wisdom was reckoned wise only when it could back itself with experience of the ages.

To those of us who were brought up in this era and who have long and with great labour applied our hearts to acquire this kind of wisdom and understanding, it is not easy to think it natural or right or even possible that aught could be hidden from us and revealed to simpler and less erudite minds, and especially to those who meet life as if they had just arrived in it. Wherefore, we explain the saying as a singular exception, due to the special privileges of the disciples on the one hand and the special dishonesty of the learned and astute of that time on the other. And for this view there is this to be said that Jesus is apparently contrasting His message with the message of the prophets. Wisdom and understanding are the same words as are used in Hosea for those who know and approve the prophet's view of God's rule in mercy and judgment. If so, Jesus is not undervaluing wisdom and understanding, but He is saying that there is both a greater message and a simpler and further-reaching way of receiving it.

Nor is this more than a deeper appreciation of a general truth, which is obscured for us by taking intellectual honesty to be a pure affair of the understanding and moral honesty to be regard to caution instructed by experience. Useful as these may be in their place, they do not reveal the unknown and unexplored—the truth we see dimly on the horizon and the purposes that pass over the horizon into the infinite. For this, in the nature of things, the meekness which commits itself wholly to discerning and the lowliness of heart which seeks nothing save to be guided, serves better than the best wisdom and understanding. What is singular in Jesus is not the way of meekness and lowliness, but the grounding it on the Father's assured love and wisdom.

Have we not to admit that our kind of understanding

blinded us to the immeasurable wonder of the world
and the endless marvel and promise of life; and that our
kind of wisdom was apt to make us seek security in
conventionality of action and comfort of possession,
rather than to be for us a trumpet call to adventure upon
the high places of the field? Nor has the present age
escaped as much as it imagines. Is it not more intent on
all kinds of insurances against mistake and calamity than
on insight and aspiration directed to hazarding the
heights of thought and enterprise?

Nor is this confined to things material. As the kind
of creation we understand is merely dividing and re-
arranging, it affords us great satisfaction to give similar
explanations everywhere. Thus dividing up by abstractions seems somehow more objective than what is
combined together in our ordinary converse with the
world and men. Yet, such converse is the only way in
which we know anything. For example, if the concern
is history, the sympathetic desire to see and understand
events and persons is regarded as little more than gossip,
while the explaining of it all as a Punch and Judy show
of movements is esteemed to be science. Or, if the
subject be literature, though its very quality is a peculiar
personal reading of life, expressed in individual felicity of
style, we are supposed to be enlightened by invoking
tendencies and grouping under -isms—Naturalism and
Classicalism and all the rest. Though taken to be both
more objective and more scientific, this only means the
stupidity of not being able to see anything except with
the spectacles of theory.

But theology affords the largest scope, because it
suffers not only from the bad spectacles of abstraction,

which sees only generalities, but can put the spectacles of the old Adam on the eyes of the new, till they see only propositions instead of inspirations, and regulations instead of the freedom of spiritual insight. Then, if meekness and lowliness of heart are admitted, it is as submissive acceptance of the opinions and directions of superior learning and wisdom, or even of superior official position.

But, if Jesus was the example He professes to be, was there ever teaching more than His from the authority of His own seeing, or action more entirely of His own deciding? Meekness is, therefore, not even accepting things as they are, but is utter consecration to seeing what God would have them to be, and lowliness of heart is following the way however hard to alter them. And still less is it accepting things as other men think they are or should be.

As this is required in face of any profound matter of truth or right, what makes Jesus unique is that this attitude is before God's love not His might, or rather His might interpreted by love not law. The utter committing of ourselves to this, whatever may come or be required, is His yoke, the yoke He himself used.

A yoke is not itself a burden, but is a way of carrying with the whole strength of the upright frame, and an easy yoke fits the shoulders and gives ungalled strength. Worrying about responsibility and fear and wavering are as sores under the yoke, or as we should say collar. This is our real distress, not the burdens of loyalty to duty, intrepidity in enterprise and faithfulness to trusts. Such burdens confirm our strength as well as constitute our worth. What we are offered is the assurance of a

purpose wise and good, which, accepted utterly, gives
rest to the soul, not in casting off its load, but in making
it light with glad acquiescence.

There are few among us not in a position to test
whether this is a genuine offer to the weary and heavy-
laden. Many a long day ago it was said, in the name of
one who had most that life could give, that "all things
are full of labour, a man cannot utter it". And, with all
our devices for lightening toil, do we feel this less? If
work is shorter and lighter, it is more monotonous,
with a new weariness to many of seeking work and not
finding it. Many have not even escaped the Preacher's
special distress of a superabundance which is itself a
burden and breeds discontent with what is either weari-
some repetitions or a striving after novelty which is a
striving after wind. We have more riches but also more
ways in which they take wings; more leisure but also
more restless ways of tearing our nerves to tatters; more
aids to being lively but also more occasions of being
down-cast. The way of the wicked is still hard, but the
way of the good, at least as most of us take it, is not very
cheerful. We are burdened by doubts and weary of all
the ways of disposing of them, burdened by what we
take to be our freedom and weary of the regulations
which would replace it. Circumstances we have greatly
altered, but how much nearer are we to rest for our
souls?

Many voices, using platform and press, propose
schemes for our ease, till they become themselves a
weariness. Change of circumstances to lighten the load
and the Government or some other impersonal power
to do most of the carrying is always the panacea, to

which might be added Abraham Lincoln's advice to take three square meals a day and keep the mind easy. But would it be rest for our souls or only slackness that we should come by in this course? Is it not something, therefore, to hear, amid the babel, so quiet a voice offering a different remedy? Not the burden, it says, wearies us, but the way we carry it.

This even good people may cherish only as a pious belief without the least expectation of finding it of practical moment. But the present distress is too real and insistent to be comforted with words, even if such conventional piety were not being vehemently denounced as the worst kind of dope, preventing men from using the only real remedy for being weary and heavy laden, which we are told is to assert themselves and cast off the load.

But while, if there is no other real succour, to this we may have to come, it would be neither lasting nor profitable. Some load we have to carry, and asserting ourselves for our own pleasing is not a light one, for in spite of the many confident voices assuring us to the contrary, it is the load upon the downward track that breaks the strength. Yet what are we to do if the sole alternative is dull routine, driven mainly by material fear, which does not allow us to rejoice in our youth or ever to be young, or our hearts to cheer us at any time, with nothing of serious interest save business as a tread-mill round?

Even classical presentations of Christianity treat the yoke as subjection and show Jesus as a woe-begone figure in a stained glass window. But was there ever anyone who bore a heavier burden with such joy and freedom as well as strength and steadfastness? And from His followers He expects the same, not offering to bear their burden but only to show them how, with rest to their souls, they can bear their own burden however heavy. Our worth is in our burden; our freedom is in the way we bear it.

Jesus is not Buddha seated in celestial calm under the fig-tree, nor as it is rather conceived, on a mountain peak, where we sit with Him in sunshine and look down upon the cloud and storm-wrack below. Neither is He Caesar on his throne, saying I am omniscient and will do all your thinking for you, and omnipotent and will take over the whole burden of your responsibilities. All things are given Him. But, through Him, they are also given us. Therefore, in meekness and lowliness, we can face what comes, not as submission to fate but as realising in it what the Apostle calls the glory of God.

Could we thus close the gap between seeing the truth and receiving it, and between knowing the right and doing it, should we not be rid of our real burden, which is not work but wavering, not high and difficult tasks but distraction among the changing and the trivial, and not alone have rest to our own souls but do something also to show the way of deliverance to the weary souls of our whole age? But it is meekness towards God's love and lowliness of heart in pursuing the way of His freedom, and so is the rest for our souls of being free from all other submissions and deferences.

CHAPTER XV

THE FELLOWSHIP OF THE SPIRIT

A MYSTERY, in our common usage, is profoundly secret and exclusively individual. But the mystery of which we are to be stewards, being of the Kingdom of God, cannot be exclusively either in ourselves or for ourselves. Stewards too are for others and not for the enjoyment merely of their own contemplations. The mystery concerns what God has in store that is beyond conceiving, but we reach out towards it as our hearts are responsive to intercourse with God's world, God's children and God Himself. In this the sons of God are led by the Spirit of God, and, as the fruit of the Spirit is love, this must be into a fellowship both with God and man, of the measureless possibilities of which even our bleared eyes have glimpses.

But here once more you may feel that we are cutting before the point, with more danger, than perhaps on any other subject, of pious unreality.

Take first "The Holy Spirit". The impression left on your mind is of a vague overwhelming potency, of which, though the general feeling is the same, there are two quite different applications: and you are not sure which you like least. In the one case, it is used to stir mass-emotion and over-ride will and judgment: and then it becomes the justification of every kind of sectarianism and idiosyncrasy in religious association. In the other, it is an almost materially operative magic of saving rites: and this demands adherence to the institutions which claim to possess them exclusively, and the surrender of all right of private judgment.

Then consider the use of "Fellowship". Is it not the chosen title for associations of cranks to justify their sense of superiority, their policies which walk on the clouds and ignore earth's hard realities, and their right to be censorious of man's amiable weaknesses and harmless peculiarities?

But words suffer degradation only in proportion to the sublimity of their true meaning; and with them also we should refuse to allow the large open spaces to become private enclosures. Nor are there many words more than "Fellowship" worth trouble to preserve for noble and unsectarian uses.

The right use of fellowship is for a society which depends on no other bond than the spirit of the whole being in each member and the freedom of each member being realised in the service of the whole. All dependence on outward organisation for its unity is a denial of its essential nature. Like other things of earth it needs outward forms, but they are for the expression and operation of a unity that exists, not for compulsion to bring it into existence. Only as each member, by being in it heart and soul, finds in its service the realisation of his own individual and personal call is it fellowship.

In this perfection it has never existed, but must wait till we are all perfected into one. Yet, even in its imperfect present realisations, it represents the true harmony in human relations, the genuine co-operation in human activities, the secret of innocent happiness, the mutual gain of possession and the best security for what is in itself essentially insecure.

Man looks on the outward appearance, and naturally puts trust in the bond of organisation and has an exaggerated esteem for what we may call the sergeant-majors of humanity, the people who seem to keep us all in step by shouting "Left", "Right". If they are equipped with political power, we fall out of step at the risk of this life; and, if with ecclesiastical, at the threat of worse still in the life to come. But what does it come to in the end?

Without railing at dignities or disallowing their usefulness in due place, we may be permitted to doubt whether the world has been as much kept in order by the dogmas and decrees of ecclesiastics, the abstractions of scientists, the armies of conquerors and the prisons and policies of rulers as by the quiet association of kindred spirits and human friendliness, rightly to be called fellowship. Is not this still our supreme bond, in spite of the violent welding into union to which the world is now being subjected? Organisation which has fellowship breathing life into its compulsions may serve a lasting as well as a high end, the more the fellowship replaces the compulsion, though now, as perhaps always, the appearance of strength may be the more with the compulsion the less it depends on anything save itself. But so it is with the rigidity of the lifeless tree, and time will tell as it has done before.

The only keeping step that ever means real progress is by each hearing for himself a music which has a common beat, though a double source, which we may call the music of the spheres and the low sad music of humanity, being thus of the spirit both of God and man.

But here you ask: Is this not getting a bit too poetical for us to say honestly what it means?

To this the answer is another question. Has not your honesty to recognise that there are some things of which even poetry is a very inadequate expression?

Are you sure that it is the merest phantasy that

> "There's not the smallest orb that thou behold'st
> But in his motion like an angel sings,
> Still quiring to the young-eyed cherubin,"

and not a great deal nearer reality than the mere motion which is all science knows about the whole galaxy of heaven? May this latter not be as inadequate as the restriction of a deaf man's knowledge of music to beating time? Nor has even this been won without humble faith in the harmony of all things. And, as for philosophy, if it have not some dim hearing of this, has it any meaning or reality?

The other strain which blends with it into a harmony of the intimacies of life is the low, sad music of humanity. It is always low, needing an attentive ear, and it may be very sad. We all do fade as a leaf and our iniquities like the wind have taken us away. Vanity of vanities, all is vanity! But sadness, turned into music, has always some melody of peace and hope. Blessed are ye that mourn, for ye shall be comforted; blessed are the merciful, for they shall obtain mercy. As we thus share it, we catch, amid the changing notes, the melody of the eternal. Has anything worthy—science or anything else—ever been done without a wonderful fellowship in service and even in sacrifice?

> "Who ne'er his bread in sorrow ate,
>   Nor passed the night's distressful hours,
> As on his bed he weeping sate,
>   He knows you not ye heavenly powers."

Dear, dear, you say, this becomes worse and worse. But again is honesty the exclusive property of dull prose and commonsense? Are we honest at all if we miss the call of the highest? And is the highest even suspected till we are in some measure attuned to both the human and the Divine harmonies?

Personally I seem to see some response to both in all progress from the lowest life. Even the development of the senses is not a mere physical process, but is an advance to meaning and value because there is a spirit seeking them from within and a Spirit giving them from without.

Yet it becomes plainer in those who have kept step by hearing both harmonies blending into one. Through them there have come to us all that is good to know and the mind to know it, all that is fair to behold and the heart to love it, all that is worth possessing and the will to acquire it. Thus what could not beforehand have entered into the heart to conceive, was won by what is man's greatest gift—the power of reaching out beyond all he sees or thinks in a world fashioned to respond.

Then the greatest blessing given to man is a Fellowship of the Spirit ever calling to him from beyond his highest aspirations. Purposes seen only by the eye vanish into night; commands assailing only the ear become empty breath; imaginations stirring only the pride of life are deceiving mirages. Only the sense of purpose beyond sight, beyond hearing, beyond conceiving, set in a Fellowship of which the human mirrors the Divine, can lead for ever onwards and upwards.

Not least of the blessings is the greater possibilities of the human fellowships by which these achievements were won; and, if so, is it mere secularising to include it all in the Fellowship of the Spirit? Is it not truer to reality to think of this as not absent from any progress in meaning and value or any heightening and glorifying of human associations, as at once their source and their inspiration, than to confine it to an ecclesiastical sphere of operation? It concerns all turning of necessity into freedom, for which end nothing is genuinely natural which is not reaching out to the spiritual and nothing effectively spiritual which is not the fulfilment of the natural. Then, if all bear in its bosom the promise of the eternal, when the evanescent is past there will have been nothing so secular that from it something of faith and hope and love will not abide.

Nor is it a mere secularisation thus to interpret the Apostolic benediction. The grace of our Lord Jesus Christ unites the love of God over all and the fellowship of the Spirit in all—so bringing into one God's rule without and within—the experiences of our lives and the aspirations of our hearts, and giving us the succour and guidance to follow a way which is of our knowledge, towards a goal which is only of God's. That it thus sums up a practical relation is at least a fuller understanding of it than that it is an authoritative Church mystery in the sense of mystery as the unknowable. Why it continues to be mystery is not because of any perplexity to the intellect, but because of the inconceivable depths of the spirit not only of God, but of man.

But once more your honesty is troubled, for, while it may have been too much occupied with merely intellectual tests, have we here any test of honesty at all? Are we not committing ourselves to the will-o'-the-wisp of the Inner Light, which has led into every kind of quagmire of craze and idiosyncrasy? What about coming and reasoning together with God? If there is truth, must we not do our best to think it out, and, if there is purpose, to define it as clearly as we can? Then, even if the supreme interest of the present is what it may become, and concentration on the past has neither guided nor inspired us in seeking it, is the wisdom and understanding to be derived from the past to be given up for this kind of mystic stuff? If the processes of the understanding have been charged with dissolving into confusing terminology, has any science, philosophy or theology ever evolved terms so technical as mysticism, or ever cultivated so deliberate, arranged and artificial a method for reaching what it regards as transcendent experience but which suggests to you rather elaborate auto-suggestion?

Mysticism, however, may mean anything from a sense of a reality beyond the seen and temporal, though only to be seen through them, which is not to be distinguished from religion, to prostration in the empty temple of the Divine Unity to be arrived at by a special process of withdrawing from sense and ultimately from thought, which it takes a great deal of logical subtlety to distinguish from pantheism. The former finds experience of the world and human fellowship a challenge to use all our powers to reason with God in order to discover His mind in them; the latter thinks that God pours in His mind as we empty ours. The belief that in this latter way we reach a more real world is akin to the idea that mathematical formulae give us a more real reality than our common observation. And, surely, religion has even less justification therein than science, for if there be a world in which God's love works and His purpose is the goal, it cannot be something for the few, but must be the world of common experience to ordinary folk in their ordinary lives.

Was it not to such people, in such circumstances, that our Lord always spoke, and what is more, from them He expected the highest, nothing in their secular vocations preventing them? Not from religious meditations and exercises, but mostly just from the common doings did He draw the parables which reveal living realities and no mere abstractions of doctrines. They speak of what meekness discerns of God in common events among ordinary people and of what lowliness of heart enters into through life's common tasks and trials. They are from a life in which eating and drinking in fellowship and enjoyment of all blessings provided is as natural as hungering and thirsting after righteousness and all the desperate hazards that involves.

No more than softness and evasion is hardness with ourselves or anyone else the way of the Spirit. The more responsive alike in joy and sorrow we are to our own spirit and the spirit of others, the more we are in fellowship with the Spirit of God. Nor is it merely in what we call spiritual fellowship, for we are nearest the Divine Spirit as we deal most kindly with the evils and defects of the human.

Let us take our Lord Himself. How much would His grace have revealed either of the love of the Father or of the fellowship of the Spirit, had it been kept apart in ecclesiastical circles from the doings of sinners just as they are, amid events just as they occur! The singular revelation is the union of God's love and the Spirit's fellowship just amid the secular events and the secular people that seem to deny both.

Yet, if happiness is in doing not in hearing only, how are we to forget the things that are behind when they will not allow themselves to be forgotten, how are we to live with undivided hearts amid our mixed human motives, and with unswerving purpose while distracted by the confused and confusing aims of mankind, and that for a purpose we have never seen, never heard of and cannot imagine?

But let us be honest with ourselves. Is not what we expect something of a formula for the understanding and of a programme for our wisdom? Especially is not this what is spoken of as the finality of Jesus Christ?

In all Scripture, there is, along with the assurance that, if we seek God, we shall, in some practical sense, find Him, the knowledge that no one by searching finds out God and that the truest worship never does more than show His skirts filling the temple. In Jesus Christ the sense of both is deepened. Thus no one ever set a higher value on what Jesus Christ had done for the knowledge of the Father than the Apostle Paul, but, while Saul the Pharisee thought he knew

God and His purposes and a straight legal road to fulfilling them, Paul the Christian, even more than Isaiah, knew that, to the end of our mortal years, we see only in part, in blurred reflexion in a mirror, darkly as in a riddle, the ways even of God's love. What he found in Jesus Christ was not the end of life's mysteries, but a relation to the Father which enabled him to forget what was behind, choose the things that excel and strive to lay hold of that for which he had been laid hold, content to see it step by step and wait God's patience for its further unfolding; and it was on this road that the fellowship of the Spirit, which was also for him the Spirit of Jesus, proved its significance and its succour.

Those who were of this Fellowship he called saints; and it is for our encouragement that they would have been canonised by no Church. Considering the crudities of their moral failures, it was a very daring thing to tell them that they were the spiritual who have to judge all things and be judged themselves of no man. So far as any recognised standard goes, none of us need hesitate to take up our position with them. Yet the Apostle lays down for them no law, no form of rite, no order of organisation, not even when the gravest abuses appeared in the observance of the Eucharist. If they discerned God's love in all their fellowship, the essential was there; if not, nothing could make it other than hypocrisy. A saint was just one open to the guidance of God's Spirit and responsive to the fellowship of human spirits, and the Apostle's confidence that no one could fail to arrive who persevered on that road, because he is even now in the Kingdom or Rule of God which brings righteousness and peace and joy in the Holy Spirit. Though it is a rule of God's world and God's creatures and not merely a state of mind within, being the one power over all and in all, it makes us right and keeps us in peace and gives us joy in all spiritual good. Though this may be so high that its manifestation may appear darkness and not light and may seem to lead through desolation and despair, yet the significance of the Christ is just to be our companion through the darkest and the worst.

As we travel this hard way, He is the truth and the life which commends unceasingly the way of the Father's high purpose with His children. And this I take to be the meaning of His sayings as He saw the end draw near. The cause of the saints was to be put to death in Him in ignominy and failure, but He said, facing this, that from henceforth the Son of Man, meaning the kingdom of the saints, would be seen coming in power with new manifestations of heavenly succour. "From henceforth" could not mean in one catastrophic event; and if it meant a new power of God's Rule and a new manifestation of God's Spirit, whatever divinity was needed for this work we should ascribe to Him, yet apart from what He wrought in meekness and lowliness of heart, it would be a mere ascription of the kind of might in which He did not trust.

CHAPTER XVI

WISDOM AND UNDERSTANDING

As wisdom and understanding were the tests of the prophetic message, our Lord is obviously not deprecating their use for their proper purpose, which is not to have revelation but to test its claims and in particular what is seen only through spectacles of traditional interpretation and theological formulation. The problems raised are many and difficult and disturbing, but, if in meekness we are whole-heartedly concerned with knowing the truth and in lowliness of heart with being led by it, there is no problem we may hesitate to face.

We need take only those which seem to affect most the foundations of the faith, such questions as miracles— in particular the Virgin Birth and the Resurrection, the Catholic faith and the many creeds, the Church and its disintegration into churches. Above all, we have to ask what is really known when we cease to build dogma upon dogma, and accept truth only on its own testimony. Though these are mainly matters of the understanding, by no kind of honesty can they be ignored.

Also there are questions of wisdom, concerned with forethought, plans and organisations. As, without them, the most impassioned belief would evaporate, these also honesty cannot evade.

First, there are historical questions. The problem for us is how to deal honestly with all inquiries without thinking that emancipation consists in seeing according to theory, and without reducing Jesus Christ to a system of historical and critical abstractions.

For a long time, miracles were presented as the chief evidence of the faith. Unfortunately, there is, for many, no point where their faith is less sure of its footing. Nor is this all. There is also, frequently, a natural dislike to the kind of compulsion to believe which says, this is the seal of the document, guaranteeing its contents, whether to your mind or not. Then the denial of all miracle seems to be a necessary vindication of freedom of judgment, whereupon it may become as dogmatic as the affirmation.

What you cannot receive to the emancipation of your mind, you must just leave in suspense. Even when you have rid yourself of the idea of being school-mastered, the healing miracles of Jesus in particular will be seen to come almost by compulsion from His compassion and to be a care for broken bodies intimately one with His care for broken souls, and so at once a credible part of His life and a great witness to the power of the spiritual over the material.

Yet this does not settle a question like the Virgin Birth. Jesus is so unique that it could easily be received were it better attested. But, were any other person in question, the testimony of a late document like Matthew and what may only be a gloss in Luke would have little weight. Some find confirmation in Paul and others deliberate rejection in John. Both are mere subtleties: and all we really do know is that, from it, neither of them derived any part of the special sonship of Jesus Christ. With Paul, as has been said, the sonship was neither physical nor metaphysical; and if with John it had something of the metaphysical this was in no way dependent on the physical. Therefore the Virgin Birth is plainly not an article of a standing or a falling faith.

The Resurrection, however, occupies a very different place, with very different testimony: and if there be any belief that should be forced upon ourselves, it would be one so intimately inwoven with the victorious faith in Jesus Christ. But, in the first place, no belief is rightly held which does not hold us; and, in the second, it is in the Gospel—the good-news of the Father from whose love neither life nor death can separate us—and not in the Resurrection, that Jesus brings life and immortality to light.

Yet how far does difficulty arise just from the attempt to compel belief? Added to this also is the fear that we should find ourselves with another Jesus than the meek and lowly in heart, one with a potent, celestial divinity over which the humanity was merely clothed as rags over coronation robes.

Regarding no historical event can we neglect the evidence: and while the different versions are not easy to reconcile, and this difference may cast doubts upon certain physical aspects of the disciples' experiences, no event was ever witnessed to by such a change from defeat to triumph and by such long and unswerving devotion in lives that showed the power of the belief as well as the conviction of it. Yet the belief would be vain unless it come to us in like manner and with like effect, which could only be by like freedom of personal persuasion. No compelled belief, even the highest, is joy and strength or other than a burden and distress.

Supposing, however, that we leave aside all other questions regarding it, is there not some response in our hearts to Peter's saying, that it was not possible that such an one should be holden of death? Surely on no other had the bondage of corruption so little hold! Nor if God approved of what He was by His mighty works in life, would this further approval by the resurrection change Him, but only show that His ways were God's patient ways, wherein He does not fail. Finally, is there not some assurance like Paul's, "It is Christ that died, nay rather that is risen again", that, "being crucified in weakness, He is raised in power", the power not of something different but just of what He was?

Yet, even in that sense you may well ask, Is He seated at the right hand of God? Has His own prophecy been fulfilled that from henceforth we should see the kingdom of the saints of the Most High coming with power? Sometimes we speak of His influence as if it were merely to be a protest against all that has happened. And if we measure by a universal typical action or rounded organisation or uncontroverted creed or anything regulated to avoid strife and error, there is no special reason for regarding His effective presence as necessary for it, more than say Mohammed for Mohammedanism. But, if it be a rule of freedom in response to the love of God and a following in the fellowship of the Spirit, a purpose beyond conceiving, is there anything to compare with His influence?

Nor is our own hope of immortality different. If our beliefs are stereotyped, our lives a fixed round of even the most admirable habits, our minds occupied with evils to be shunned and dangers to be escaped, in short if we have reached finality in any way, immortality could only promise an endlessly weary round of dull monotony. But if the love of God is the assurance that we cannot fall out of an endless purpose, and that neither life nor death can separate from it, it must also give a life so large that we can never exhaust its wonder. Even now by its light the wonder of this world is unceasing and the deep humanities only need the response of our souls to be without limit. Yet these seem only a slight lifting of the veil, the beckoning of an inconceivable and endless purpose. Nor should we need in it any other blessedness than what the Apostle hoped for, which is that we may know as fully the rule of love in all, as now we trust dimly that it knows us.

Second, the dogmatic questions—Of all this can we have anything like a theology? How far can understanding go in formulating and organising our beliefs?

As it has been my business for a good part of a fairly long life-time to read and ponder on such matters, possibly you may have a right to ask me, what, when we cease to build assumption, does it, in honesty, amount to? And possibly, in honesty, I should have to say, what has already been said about Biology when it ceases to build theory upon theory, that what we know on the testimony of its own witness is very little. Perhaps too the reason may be the same in both cases, that the result has been so small because the methods were not suited to the subjects. Biology has overlooked the unity of life and its characteristic quality of being directed, in however dim a way, by its own knowledge, on its own motive and to its own ends. So Theology can forget that it deals with one relation to God in one fellowship and for one endless purpose, unfolding itself, and that only brokenly, to the spirit of love: and has sought finality by invoking the past to fix formulas and decide authorities. In both cases we have to deal with a living organism to be understood as we see it to be one, not with mere mechanical coherence which we can take to pieces and put together again.

Then the understanding ceases to be the servant of vision and takes to school-mastering it, telling it both how to look and what to see.

Of this result the most notable example is in those who crucified Jesus. They had fixed all their views in the authority of the past. On the ground of it, they developed a traditional casuistry about externals and ignored the source of all morality in the heart. Any living word of God was naturally set at naught by such tradition: and as Jesus had nothing else, His offence was greatest. The religious institutions too, being tradition's chief buttress, became religion's supreme interest, and nothing was wrong by which any who questioned their authority or menaced their power and dignity were to be suppressed—the end justifying the means.

Should we, in like manner, ever come to think God's ends to be of our discerning, His work of our compassing, His fellowship of our sustaining and His approval according to our judging, that we do it in the name of Christ will not prevent us from being of those who crucify Him.

Also, though conceived to be in the service of Christ, theological understanding may, as of old, lay on us unnecessary burdens as well as be the wong way of carrying the right ones. It too can provide abstractions which seem to be more objective because independent of the kind of persons we are and the kind of experience we have. To save them from the influence of the common speech, which is steeped in personal intercourse with men and things, they are given names from Greek which have long been emancipated from the menial tasks of common life, though truth, even the highest, is only learned and verified in the common intercourse expressed in the common speech. Should the Lord answer this plague of terminology, would it not be out of the whirlwind, saying, "Who is this that darkeneth counsel with words without knowledge?"

Yet the worst fault of all the –ologies—Christology, Pneumatology, Soteriology, Ecclesiology and the rest —is that they isolate and divide what should be one in itself and the source of unity in all. Instead, we can have such a distinction as objective and subjective Soteriology, as if the whole question were not how God acts so as to stir our response and we respond so as to discover it to be God's act. Then, we have justification, which, isolated, becomes mere acquittal; and regeneration which, isolated, works like bleaching powder; and sanctification which, isolated, makes grace like a mechanical elevator. This is what understanding reaches when working on its own; whereas meekness and lowliness of heart sees it all as one in the love of the Father and the Fellowship of His Spirit.

Another division is between Christian doctrine and Christian ethics, and, in the ethics, between the individual and the community. But ethics is specially Christian only because of the doctrine; and there is a sense in which we could say that the doctrine is singular only because of the ethics. Moreover, in respect of both, though, as has been said, religion is what man does with his solitariness, for the freedom wherewith Christ set us free is not to be won anywhere than in our own minds and hearts and consciences, yet his fellowship is not something added to the individual but is an essential part of himself. The more he is himself is he truly in it, and the more he is in it is he truly himself.

Nevertheless, if we cease to be God's children in God's family or fail to arrive at it, and are merely members of a corporation of which the last idea would be that he that is spiritual judges all things and himself is judged of no man, but, on the contrary, that he is to be judged and not judge, the most vehement denial of law does not prevent the introduction of the legal spirit with its denials and its dictations. The law of commandments contained in ordinances does not need to be formulated as a body of casuistry, recognised in the same way as judicial precedent, in order to be a very effective turning of Christianity into a new law. Even what is called Moral Theology, however much it may go beyond the outward act than the usual casuistry, is still apt to call external sins mortal and sins of the heart venial, and, in its efforts to provide rules of wisdom and understanding, it is apt to come short of the insight of the meek and lowly in heart. As the most rigid prescript can be overtaken while the liberty of the spiritual man in Christ Jesus cannot, the tendency to provide prescript and accept it is ever with us. The temper of law may even masquerade as liberty, the issuing of commands as the giving of counsel, and the domination of the movement as the individual's personal guidance.

With this goes the tendency of our finite minds to divide in order to rule, by turning helpful distinctions into unhelpful divisions. In no subject is this more common than in Theology. In it, as in other spheres, we should learn from those who have gone before us, and not least from their mistakes. Yet the elaborate discussions in theological treatises are only misleading, the masses of erudition only a burden, and the endless discussions of errors no illumination. Compendiums may be useful, but are not contributions to theology.

Theology should be systematic thinking, not to force everything into a system, but to set forth in order the relations as well as the significance of our highest intuitions. For this, Jesus is the ultimate authority because the truth is so manifested in Him that it needs no other appeal, and not because we should set Him among outward authorities, even if it be over them. He spoke with the authority of truth manifest to all who did not meet its appeal with hypocrisy; and He neither used authorities nor was one. To be His disciples in this is so to present the truth that, if men will to do the will of God, they will know the doctrine.

But even to approach this, we must never forget that we are dealing at once with an outward order independent of us and with our inward persuasion of it, and, in that persuasion, at once with our own solitary meditation and resolve and with intimate fellowship with all God's children, and at once also with overcoming the world and possessing it. Every distinction in this which cuts deep enough to divide changes as it were the physiology of life into the anatomy of death. Our concern is not God alone or the world alone or man alone or Jesus or the Spirit alone, but one Rule of the Father, manifest in each of us being sons in the fellowship of His Spirit, through the grace of our Lord Jesus Christ.

For this, nothing that man has thought or done may be irrelevant, but Scripture in particular will ever be more fully revelation as it ceases to be a dictation of beliefs and code of directions and becomes the counsel of God, to be received and proved only as we make it our own.

Nor is it really different with the true Church. Of both it may be thought that by this liberty we are sapping their power. Yet it is precisely as they are made legal authorities imposed on us that we can manipulate them to say what we would, just as it is adherence to the letter of the law which is the main support for applications the legislator never intended.

CHAPTER XVII

THE CATHOLIC FAITH AND
THE CONFESSIONS

Here we come to the still greater difficulty of dogmas as creeds. If there be something which marks Christianity as a whole, there must be something to be described as the Catholic Faith. But, when this is understood as a particular creed, we are using Catholic no longer in its original sense of the quality of a Christian fellowship, but as the exclusive claim of a particular society, which is none the less a denomination for being the largest and most ancient. As many are called and few chosen, largeness guarantees neither truth nor order; and, seeing how old is error and how painful is progress, antiquity may only be enduring from stagnation and impressive from remoteness. But if neither the Catholic nor any other confession is more than the profession of a denomination and mostly of its clerical leaders, are not creeds, by their very nature, divisive?

Nothing, however, that is distinctive need be divisive; and we might be nearer, if we better understood our differences and the historical causes of their origin.

There is, as the most notable example, the reason why the Christian Faith became a new law and a new ritual and took the form of imposed dogma. Those converts who had never had the training of the Old Testament dispensation did not escape the need of it by becoming nominally Christian; and as the order of the Church had more and more to replace the order of the State, the imposition of its creed as State law seemed to be a way of peace and quiet. The idea of the Father, Son and Spirit as one substance was a more direct reply to polytheism than seeing the Father in the Son; and it also made grace easy to conceive through rites with the efficacy of omnipotence, to which the sense of mystery helped to give a sense of depth.

The necessity of receiving spiritual impressions in material forms is a very old story, and, if at a time when no other way was possible, this form of creed did preserve the essentials of the worship of one God, it deserves our regard. Yet if we do not now require it, we are not called to force it upon ourselves, because the greatest utility for the time does nothing to prove eternal validity. We may even think it was super-subtlety in the Reformers to seek to find in the early creeds the spiritual significance of Jesus and reconciliation to the Father: and we may have to say that we see in them only the authority of Church mysteries and the potency of mystic rites: and that this is not to us the significance of the Incarnation. With a historical mind and the knowledge that, in the same circumstances, we should have renounced the same errors in the same forms, it is doubtless possible to repeat even the Athanasian Creed with honesty. Yet we may be allowed to feel relief when our common confession is the Church's central creed, which is the Lord's Prayer.

Still are there not other confessions Churches are supposed to believe? And if so, can acceptance be either in freedom or honesty? Is it not accompanied by subtleties which are sophistic and subjections which are slavish?

Yet is the knot really cut by dispensing with written formulas? Some kind of traditional creed must be the assumption of any institution which goes back to the origins of Christianity; and this may be more arbitrary and more exacting. Were we even to start a Church of our own, we should still have to defer to the past and seek accord with other people.

Confessions are part of our external heredity, which, like our personal heredity, we can neither utterly reject nor simply accept, but have to travel through as well as go beyond. With the faith of our fathers we have to wrestle till at break of day it bless us, even if some halt in our freedom still betrays the agony of the night.

What then is the value of the confessions Churches are supposed to receive? and, to bring the matter to a point, you say, What about your own? You seem to have heard of a very elaborate confession called the Westminster, which among many other dubious matters, has a covenant made with Adam and a very high doctrine of election, which do not seem much in accord with my own views.

Two questions here arise which are not distinct, nor, if history has meaning for us and we have to work with other people, is thought about them or even compromise with them to be dismissed as sophistry.

There are four different purposes confessions may be meant to serve.

The first we may call apologetic. They are to justify singularity in faith and practice by explaining it and defending it. The Augsburg is called The Apology and the Gallican might have been named the same. By giving expression to common conviction, common fellowship and common purpose, they did notable service in times of stress: and they have made themselves a history which those who have been fashioned by it surely need not repudiate on matters of detail.

The second purpose is didactic, that is, for instruction: and the special form is the catechism. The doubt here is about the means and not about the end. Even if unity be the ultimate end, while seeking it by instruction is surely to be commended, dogmatic affirmation may not be the best instruction.

The third purpose is polemical, that is, for refutation of error. Such are all the early Creeds: and we mistake them if we expect to find in them a presentation of the whole faith. Of Protestant confessions the most marked example is the Decrees of the Synod of Dort; and the Roman Decrees of Trent, though also for enforcing uniformity, are, in the spirit which informs it through-out, polemical. Here again the doubt is more about the way of serving the end and the temper in following it, than the end itself.

The last purpose is the eirenical, that is for making peace and imposing unity. Besides the Decrees of Trent, this was the express purpose of the Thirty-nine Articles and the Westminster Confession. Here the question above all else is the temper. To promote unity by bringing us to one mind is an end to be warmly approved; to seek to create union by compelling us to agreement, has, as a matter of fact, been among the most divisive forces in history.

Yet to many the one object of a confession is to create

a uniformity of faith by being imposed verbatim and literatim; and to profess any acceptance of it without swallowing it whole, package as well as medicine, is held to be dishonest. But if the first question is, are we in accord with the general purpose? the second is, how far may we regard the rest as matters of history to be interpreted historically? Only with very full recognition of the latter could an honest person accept a creed. Of the churches which possess them, the Anglican has made it plain by its ordinary method of precedent and the Presbyterian by its usual method of written declarations that no literal adhesion is intended. To both their confessions are historical documents which, unless we must be forever changing them and thereby losing touch with the history they embody, must be interpreted by substance and not by form. Yet, even so, as a means of enforcing uniformity, we have only to think of the vast variety of opinions in the Presbyterian Churches, and the still greater in the Episcopal, to know how little is its value. As imposed law, the creeds have mostly caused outward bitterness and inward perplexity of conscience. In few ways have we made more progress in what concerns our peace than in discovering what great differences in doctrine can be consistent with true fellowship of the Spirit, and if a creed be used to insist on orthodox docility, the end would no more be unity than it would be freedom.

But, it may be said, is it not mere antiquarianism to have this fuss about ancient documents? Why not have a modern confession, which would say just what we believe and no more, and be a new apology to a hostile world?

Unfortunately you cannot say "Go to, let us indite a confession!" Great confessions need great occasions in great times, when, with concern for the things of the spirit, the thoughts of many hearts are revealed: while modern confessions, with their balanced intellectual compromises, are all still-born. Therefore, the question is whether, with right allowance for change, which may be either by the general evidence of action or by particular expression of attitude, our confessions may do something more than remind us of the hole of the pit from which we were digged and afford still some outline of our particular kind of piety.

Yet, you still ask, is this more than lip service? The simplest way, you say, is to take my own case. The covenant theology we may allow was just the first step towards a historical outlook, seeing that we had the same stage in political philosophy: and, if we have reached a more historical view, it may be regarded as fulfilment not contradiction. But what about election and everything determined by the fiat and foreknowledge of God, which dominates the Westminster Confession from first to last? In view of what I have already said about this as the same kind of over-simplification as the mechanical theory of science, can it have for me any real significance?

That it has been found a burden to many is shown by the fact that it is usually the first element in the confession to be modified, though generally without seeing how much the modification is a transformation. Yet of the continued attachment to it the explanation is that people regard chiefly the type of piety and this remains in essentials unchanged, it being only a deeper understanding of the Divine Sovereignty and not a denial of it to see that its very quality and operation is to have the patience of wise love, which incarnates itself in One who is meek and lowly in heart in order to guide by counsel and win us as children, not control us as marionettes.

This we cherish as long as we bear in mind that the one security worse than our own steadfastness of purpose for being able to carry through to the end is to expect to be carried along on a wave of emotion. Extreme Calvinism I never came across, for I knew it only among a race who, whether for thought or action, divided humanity into men who went to sea and muffs who stayed at home, and for whom the sovereignty of God meant the assurance of being able to face all storms, and seek no harbour of refuge. Nor had they any idea of having to work up the salvation of their souls. The real opposite of the dogma of Divine Sovereignty is striving and crying instead of turning in simplicity and trust to God. Left to itself most English religion accepts it in this form, and, if so, and the substance is right, we may still retain some regard for the form as showing the road we have travelled.

The form served its purpose in its time, doing something for the new venture in religious liberty like what the mechanical theory did for science and what the authority of the Church did in the first encounter with Paganism. All were over-simplifications, and not least a rigid doctrine of election and predestination. The help was in ruling out complication when in the valley of decision. So far is the Westminster Confession from being singular in this doctrine, except in emphasis, that all early Protestant Confessions have the same general outlook, without which people would have thought they had been brought out of a Church that guaranteed doctrine, had the saving rites and claimed a control of salvation, in order to perish in the wilderness. But a definite decree settled by God, of definite salvation managed by God, and definite control guaranteeing doctrine and determining organisation, which, if it were called the Election of Grace, had all the fixity of a decision of power, seemed no bad substitute. Time has made vanity of much of this assurance, because love does not control like power. Yet the question for us still is whether love is not the only power in the end to lead us into all truth and lift us up to the fullness of fellowship, and whether what was wrong in the expectation was only that man imposed upon it his hasty and violent ways, not that in the end any of us can say aught except, "In Thee O Lord have I trusted".

CHAPTER XVIII

THE CHURCH AND THE CHURCHES

No action is right without inward honesty, but also inward honesty cannot long be maintained without the support of outward action. Hypocrisy arises because, when we do not bring our conduct into accord with our conscience, we tend to bring our conscience into accord with our conduct; and aspirations and inspirations turn to self-delusions if they remain aspirations and inspirations without being applied to earth's common tasks and every-day problems. To the Apostle, obedience to the heavenly vision was not by cherishing rapt meditations but by a toilsome round of preaching on the well-worn theme that men should repent and turn to God and do works meet for repentance. The vision gave insight, devotion and high concern to the service; and the service gave reality and continuance to the vision.

What our heavenly vision is determines for us our whole attitude to life and history: and, with that, the value of all human institutions. To one person, the supreme end is to have the right beliefs accepted and the right actions done, it matters less how: and then the authority of the institution is itself the fulfilment of the vision. To another, the whole value of belief is in personal conviction of its truth and of action in personal judgment of its righteousness and personal dedication to its performance: and then the institution is only a means to the freedom of personal discernment and consecration, and all imposed order at best an imperfect and passing means.

As the side we take determines, in practice as well as theory, our views of the ends and methods of all human associations, the first question for our honesty is to determine which vision we cherish. While the difference affects all co-operation with others, it specially determines our view of the State and the Church, and until we know on which side we stand discussion of them is waste of breath.

On the former view, while it would be thought well to have all possible individual consent, to depend on it is deemed weakness, and the hope of all unity and order is by subjection to an external authority.

To-day the prevailing vision is an unassailable political authority, with individual judgment as the enemy, which is to be absolute within the nation's own frontiers and able to make its will felt in any way that is profitable beyond them.

To counter this kind of universal dominion, others have the vision of a super-state, able to loose the bonds of kings, with righteousness as the girdle of its loins.

With this we naturally have an extension of the State idea of compulsion, the whole interest being in getting things done, with less concern about why they are done. Both conceptions, however, are a very ancient story which is not encouraging to the hope that such powers have eternal foundations. Even now will organisation work without an inspiring soul, which, if we use the term widely enough, we can call a Church?

But the Church again is regarded as an organisation

able to dictate belief and prescribe conduct. And it is true that the world was never as near a super-state able to enforce peace and allow profitable intercourse, as when it had such backing. For this the heavenly vision is a united organisation, which, if it cannot impose one belief, can at least impose one confession; and if it cannot bring peace and good-will, can at least enforce the actions that should go with them.

Essentially, however, this is a State ideal. Wherefore, its first object is unity, sectarianism in the Church being the same source of weakness as rebellion in the State. Schism is the supreme iniquity as it has reduced what might be the most influential of all institutions to its present feeble condition. Wherefore, even if there is no longer one fold, must we not take the largest, and return to it, if necessary in the white sheet of the penitent?

Under the sense of the chaos around us, any hope of order has its attraction. Yet, for my part, I can find no sense in life and no meaning in history on the view that God is as much concerned with correct doctrine, approved action and regulated institution as man is. To have made us all infallible in every judgment and un-deviating in every action would surely have been child's play for His omnipotence. But if the sole perfect order be the freedom of God's children, and it involve knowing God's mind of our own insight and doing His will of our own discernment and consecration and having a relation to others which is a fellowship mutual both with God and man, and, that, in the end, God will not be content with less, surely we can see, dimly at least, the necessity for the long hard way man has had to travel. Even the losses of his cherished possessions and

o   H

the uncertainty of life, if they prevent him from settling down in the lower order, may be as necessary as the removing of a child's playthings when the time comes for him to put away childish things. And among the possessions and safeguards which have to be sacrificed might well be the unity, material prosperity and power of the visible Church, as well as the stability of the State.

True unity we can have only when the prayer is fulfilled that "They all may be one as I and the Father are one". Though often quoted in support of union by submission to authority, such union might not even forward it, as differences even in the most authoritarian institutions, and not least Churches, amply show. Its only fulfilment is the new covenant, which Jesus sealed with His blood, that no one need say to his brother, Know the Lord for all know Him, or direct his conduct for God has written His law on all hearts. This and nothing short of it is the Rule or Kingdom of God.

As it has to do with the whole world order, we cannot exclude any human interest, public or private, and make it merely an affair of the Church. But, as the Church, we may assume, is the special organ of the Kingdom of God and its methods should be specially determined by the Fellowship of His Spirit, with it we begin.

Originally the term translated Church did not mean an institution, but was applied to the fellowship of those who were not disobedient to the heavenly vision of the Rule of the Father, in harmony of thought and purpose, which was summed up as loving Christ's appearing. Yet so long as we are in the body, we cannot be independent of forms and organisations and ceremonies, and customs in respect of them. Even our Lord went to the synagogue on the Sabbath as His custom was. Nor was such a custom ever more necessary than in our restless age. Though unfortunately customs and institutions by themselves are apt to fail just when most needed, yet, if not by themselves but sought for purposes beyond themselves, they may be our required succour: and honesty with our limitations should compel us to admit the need. Religious societies may differ in value as in other respects, but no one maintains a robust religious life unconnected with any of them.

None the less Jesus created something far greater than the Church; and the watershed of our ideas about the Church is determined by whether we regard the Church as in itself an end or only a very imperfect and, for that reason, necessarily changing means to a higher end.

Were it only an organisation Jesus founded, were it the largest beneath the stars, what sense would there then be in speaking of Him as manifesting the order by which and for which all things were created? This is not of size but of quality, and is true only of an order founded on the love of God and built up by the Fellowship of His Spirit. So far as the Church is that, it is at least a shadow of the perfect order to come, wherein is embodied all harmony not only on earth but in all the heavens.

Jesus no doubt knew that an organisation would arise, but He laid down no rules for it, except to insist that it should not over-ride its true purpose, which is to be an order in which God alone is our teacher and we call no man Rabbi and Christ is our sole leader and His followers are all brethren, willing to be first in service and last in honour. Wherefore, necessary as the visible organisation may be, defects which show it to be of time and not of eternity may be part of God's plan for preventing us from making it a material and worldly dominion, and so a facile way of walking by things seen and temporal, and not our most helpful reminder of the unseen and eternal.

There is a parallel in the history of Israel. Out of the divisions which weakened it as a nation arose the idea of a spiritual Israel, and with it came the whole prophetic revelation. Similarly, may it not be that God has allowed outward unity to be broken up, that we may be driven to seek what would make us truly one as Christ is one with the Father? Wherefore, while our divisions in themselves are to be deplored, yet considering what human nature is, and ecclesiastical human nature in particular, the situation may not be so deplorable as it would have been had there been no meekness before God which was not at all meek before man.

Its value may be just in testing whether we live in the unseen or the things seen and our fellowship a deep reality of the spirit of man and the Spirit of God or only a superficial affair of names, similarity of types and outward conformities.

No Church, even at its best, is any adequate manifestation of what the Fellowship of the Spirit should be. But we are not thereby set free from concern with it even at its worst. Our interest in it should be like an artist's in his work. He is a poor artist who can realise anything approaching his vision, but he will soon have no vision at all unless he do his best not only in spite of failures, but through failures, to realise it.

As the Church should never be the end, but only the very imperfect means for realising on earth the Fellowship of the Spirit, we should not even try to persuade ourselves that its limitations and failures are other than limitations and failures, even if they may seem to be ecclesiastical excellencies. Yet, if we serve the visible fellowship loyally and faithfully to make it an ever better reflexion of the spiritual, there may be for us no form of the Church which does not derive some glory from the vision of its purpose, and no form of serving it which does not help to exalt the vision and keep it from fading. If to us the spiritual order appears as the final order not of the Church alone but of the world, the Church will not appear to us as a finished or even a separate corporation. Yet as man's most conscious fellowship, in seeking to realise the Fellowship of the Spirit, it should be no less cherished because human and imperfect, being glorified precisely by what, though working in it, is far beyond it.

But, you may say, that there is no Church, only churches.

If the Church is first of all the order of freedom, it is exposed to the hazards of division as no other order; and, as Christianity was itself a schism from Judaism, there must be occasions when, with all charity, loyalty to the order for which the Church stands may both justify and require separation. Among the most galling burdens from which Christ's yoke promised deliverance were the meticulous rites and regulations of the Church, and among the greatest evils through which the Cross commends God's love was the burden of its religion. His deadly opponent was not irreligion but bad religion, and bad for Him meant mainly formal, ceremonial and traditional. Against this, even invoking His own name is not a guarantee; and, supposing there is a sin of schism, is it in those who would not be entangled in this yoke of bondage or in those who impose it? Anyhow a spiritual faithfulness which maintains the liberty wherewith Christ sets us free cannot always be wrong against a material authority which denies it.

As with differences in opinion, differences about organisation may be due just to our human limitations: and both alike should present occasion, not for alienation, strife and bitterness, but for giving more earnest heed to the unity of the spirit in the bonds of love. A true family recognises independence and individuality of service as a bond not an alienation, and no success or failure in following one's own call justifies receiving patronage from one member or extending it to another. Wherefore, though above all other orders the household of faith cultivates the independent mind and action which may lead to differences, it should also in a supreme degree have the spirit of love and fellowship to make them of mutual benefit and keep them from hardening into alienation and perpetual divergence.

In that case, then, you may say, if it has come to inward alienations as well as outward separations, plainly this spirit has been lacking. And doubtless it has. But all the more it may be required in us in dealing with them when they do happen. Outward separations have too often reflected the absence of inward fellowship. Like other shortcomings they arise from the imperfections of human nature. But what else requires the exercise of charity? If we are to be charitable only when no one has made mistakes and allow nothing for our possible bias as to who made them, the demands upon us would be small.

The value of these outward divisions may just be to test whether our fellowship is a mere matter of names or embodies a sympathy and understanding both human and divine. If the substance of unity is lost, that the semblance of union should no longer cloak it may be gain to reality and self-knowledge. The question is not, granting that we were all perfect, what would the form of the Church be, but, granting we are what we are, are our divisions a greater evil than enforced union? Might not such a Church have been a political and a personal as well as a religious tyranny, still further than we are from any real Fellowship of the Spirit, and less conscious of its distance? Also might not the ecclesiastical despot, ruling over an undivided and utterly subject realm, have been a more deadly suppressor of every kind of freedom, with a slavery reaching into the depths of the soul, than the worst political autocrat?

Union, therefore, is not so all-important that in any and every way we should seek it. Yet it may be very important sought in the right way, and the seeking it in the right way may be more important still.

The right way is to seek first unity, and hope from it for union. To begin by trying to patch up the organisation and trust it to amend the spirit may not even be the shortest way and is certainly not the most persuasive. To expect us to be responsive to the kind of recognition which says, "You are at present an alien and an outcast, but I shall be ready to greet you as a brother as soon as our ecclesiastical leaders have patched up an agreement", is not taking account either of what is best in us or what is worst. If we have our loyalties, even if not the most enlightened, we cannot dispose of them in this fashion.

What we have first to do is to cultivate the Fellowship of the Spirit and trust that outward union may come out of it. All increase of intercourse is to be welcomed to this end: nor is there much doubt of good fruit already in greater friendship and understanding.

Yet the best means of all for unity of fellowship is not available. Of all ways of showing how the love of the Father in the life without and the Fellowship of the Spirit within is one in the grace of Christ the greatest is the sacrament in which the symbols used sanctify the whole material life and make it transparently radiant with the spiritual. This is not a rite of any church, or for that matter of the Church at all, but expresses the nature of the Fellowship, and should never be observed without inviting all who acknowledge it to partake. That in the name of the Carpenter of Nazareth it should be made the basis of a sacerdotal and hierarchical exclusiveness is perhaps as sad a perversion of the original purpose as anything in history. Yet there we must leave it for it is no appropriate subject for controversy. Yet not discerning the Lord's body among the rich and the poor was of old the way of drinking condemnation. So it may be to-day among distinctions of denominations; and perhaps denominations have been appointed just to prove whether our fellowship has a better way of recognising one another than the repetition of shibboleths, and is Christian enough to embrace them. Yet though, in matters of fellowship, it is always denial that has to justify itself, any kind of denial is better than gracious permission. Fellowship is not allowing others to partake of the crumbs which fall from our particular table, but is the same freedom and friendship as Jesus used even when dining with publicans and sinners. And if we are honestly shocked by the queer company in which this might land us, honesty should also compel us to realise that the same Providence which suffers us, may well suffer many queer creatures besides.

CHAPTER XIX

OUTWARD FREEDOM

As the Kingdom of God is the whole final order and not a new ecclesiastical institution, the vision of its freedom applies to all our associations. Of these the most dominant at least is the State. But, dress it up as we may, the method of the State, in the end, is compulsion of the weaker by the stronger: and is not that the direct opposite of the method of the Kingdom?

In two ways, however, the heavenly vision of an order secure in honesty of conviction and freedom of action has affected the idea of the State. One is by modification of its method, and the other is by limitation of its sphere. The former involves not merely the rights of minorities but equal justice between men simply as men, along with increasing reliance on the consent and co-operation of all, both for the State's maintenance and for its working. The other involves the rights not only of conscience but of the organisations which spring from it to exist in independence of the State: and the logical outcome of the position would be that the State is only a temporary necessity till a people learns to rule itself.

To-day we have vehement reaction from both. The method of the State is more than ever the display of force with no limits set either by creed or conscience to its application.

Yet the only real danger is in ourselves, for, in the end

freedom is not secured by constitutions, but by those to whom it is dearer than life: and, so long as it has this value for us, by nothing can we be enslaved. When, however, we come to think of freedom as mere liberty to choose our own way of happiness, mainly material, there is always a point, much short of the price of life, where it becomes "too dear for our possessing". Only if there is a spiritual conviction that man's true worth is in his responsibility and the supreme value of freedom the right and power to exercise it, is no sacrifice for freedom too great.

A question similar to that between the inward fellowship and the Church is the relation between freedom in the soul and in the State. No outward constraint, it may be, can take our inward freedom from us, yet there might be a kind of submission to it that does.

Of opposite views and their effect, we have a large-scale illustration in Lutheranism and Calvinism. To Luther it appeared that freedom could be maintained, if not within our own hearts, at least within our own gates, while freedom in the State should be left for God and the rulers to settle between them. Calvin also thought that freedom could and should be maintained within in spite of all outward dominion, yet only on condition of doing our utmost to establish it without. With this went different ideas of salvation. To Lutheranism salvation was in the main personal edification for inward freedom, to Calvinism it was primarily being called to serve the glory of God in the world without as well as our hearts within.

Of the consequences there are few greater examples in history of the power of ideas.

Whether Luther represented Germany or Germany echoed Luther or there was something of both, for centuries, if the Germans could have freedom of thought, freedom of action mattered little. To-day action is used to drill thought, and this is the only aspect of its tyranny which so far has raised opposition. In other matters there is a surrender to the rulers inconceivable in any country holding Calvin's persuasion about freedom. Again it may be difficult to say how far Calvin created this and how far he only reflected it, yet he did not influence in this matter his own country less because it cast him out, nor the English-speaking races less because he came not with peace but a sword.

Gardiner the historian ascribes the English constitution directly to his influence. "It is ", he says, "beyond all question the work of Presbyterianism." Yet, if he be right, the elements most important were omitted. Though the Englishman, he adds, has shouted for aristocracy and for democracy, the Presbyterian idea of equality he never has understood and never will. But this equality of the spiritual man was the sole ground put forward for his equal rights in the State, which went if not with equal duties at least with equal claims upon his duty. And, without such right and duty, why should not the weakest go to the wall? And a still better bulwark for the democracy was also omitted with the failure to take over the religious conception of office. This is not election to privileged superiority, but the call of God, through the people, to special duties and responsibilities before Him alone. This may seem rather in the clouds, but surely we could find a way nearer calling leaders because God has already called them by the needed gifts and graces, and putting them forward in spite of themselves, than the present way of choosing them, like tooth pastes, because their own advertisements speak well of them. And if their number should be less, like the Sibylline books, their value might be more.

Yet Presbyterianism almost perished in giving birth to the constitution: and perhaps the reason was that it was more akin at the time to a state constitution which would take the Kingdom of Heaven by violence than to the fellowship which has room for the endless variety of mankind and God's infinite patience in winning them to their true individual quality as His children. And it may be that even the English constitution has survived less by the wisdom and understanding of schemes like Calvin's constitution at Geneva than by something more akin to the revelation granted to babes.

The English are the best diplomatists, a Russian is reported to have said, because the French are so logical that all know where they will arrive, the Germans so systematic that the building shouts its end from the foundation, the Russians so prolific in schemes that all know none will be executed, but no one knows what the English are thinking because they do not know themselves.

This is probably irony, but it might be praise. Cromwell said he was never promised guidance till he needed it: and with due awareness of our ignorance of the future, should we expect it sooner? Might this not be a sound secular version of meekness as readiness to see things as they are when they are, and of lowliness of heart as then doing the best we can with them as we see how?

Unfortunately imitative education, the contagion of a plague of Atlases who think their shoulders broad enough to carry the world, the willingness of people to hand over their share of the burden to those ready to take it, and with this the self-approval which comes to common mortals when a seat in parliament is regarded as a seat on Olympus, are making us think that we should be as logical as the French, as systematic as the Germans, as subtle as the Italians, with the usual effect of imitations, that they are much better at copying defects than virtues. The result is perilous departure from the only real wisdom given to man of meeting whatsoever comes with robust uprightness and simple courage, as the occasion demands and the day declares, for what is not even very good as human devices. We consult many physicians who prescribe for evils which may not come or come in a form not expected, and, after spending all our living, there is the old result of being nothing better.

Among other prescriptions is artificial bathing in the sunshine of our own virtues. Instead of the old way of thinking misrepresentation rather a tribute, we have come to agreement with Uncle Toby, that, while it is a very unpleasant thing to have to praise oneself, it is better than doing a good deed and getting no praise for it at all. Yet if it is not wisdom that lifts up the voice in the street, what can be said of the effort to command the air!

If we do not know of ourselves how little we know, we might learn a little from history. Has any great human pretence ever fulfilled its expectations, at least in its own way? Has not much that has been thought bad been good and good bad? Take the autocrats. Will they end by establishing autocracies or larger freedom? Perhaps they are needed for a time to pull down and pluck up. Nor can we be sure that some things we in our blindness call disaster are not needed to prepare for a higher, freer order. Honesty requires us to have an open mind, but an open mind does not lose faith that freedom and honesty are one and that, in the end, the gates of Hades cannot prevail against it. There was once a cause which seemed to be buried in the grave of a peasant crucified as a criminal, which came again as no other with power from above.

With this we should be ready to face all claims, even though it lead us into politics itself. The State may not even be plainly a means towards the Rule of God, but a very mixed historical product, apt to tempt even the wary into dubious devices. So many and so deceiving are the possibilities that the only way of escape is overcoming them with good. But this is true of every sphere and the question of what is due consideration and what weak concession may still beset most of us everywhere, yet, with a meekness which has no concern except to see the way and a lowliness of heart which has no interest except to follow it, we may confidently trust that there is no situation on earth wherein we shall not be helped to see and follow the higher way of what the Apostle calls the things that excel.

But even outward freedom is not determined merely by the form of the political rule. It requires a rule that is both free and has room for freedom, and a totalitarian elected parliament would differ from a totalitarian autocrat only by less efficiency and not by less interference. A free country is one in which the responsibility of the individual is the main direction and efficiency. But to this end, as the method of the State is compulsion, its sphere should be limited to what can be so controlled, and its glory should be in the large scope it offers for more intimate and more spiritual associations, the only condition being that, as the method of the State must rule in material things, no spiritual interest may involve itself more in material possessions than is absolutely necessary for its purpose.

Of all these associations the Church presents the gravest problem. The Reformation view that the religious life is not contemplations, exercises and rites, but the common life rightly lived, led everywhere to the establishment of the Church as the organ of the State for the service of the common life. As their methods tend to conflict, the running has not been smooth, and though secular and sacred may not without disaster be divorced, to save the methods of both Church and State from hurtful complications the form of their association would need to be changed from the State's compulsion as a means to the Church's freedom as an end.

At present any relation of Church and State would seem to be easy. There being much division, one section can be used to balance the other: and religion anyhow is not a very burning interest. But religion has a way of waking up to renewed vigour and dominating all other interests. What may then happen both to civil and religious liberty? If the Church then took to uniting, as, for example, it has in Scotland, it would require the highest wisdom and forbearance in restricting itself rigidly to its own sphere of spiritual freedom were it not to be a menace and a tyranny.

If we take the State as every kind of rule by outward order and the Church as what trusts only to spiritual freedom, it would seem plainly to be progress as the latter more fully serves and the former is less required. Yet an ecclesiastical state would be the worst form of transferring compulsion where it does not belong.

The other great association is the family, though the Church is more itself the more it is the family and the less it is the State. Yet the family above all raises the problem for our freedom and our honesty of how we have both most fully and most securely in loyalty to our natural ties and responsibilities.

The family is related both to the Church and to the State in the larger sense just given them.

No tie is so unchangeable as parent and child, brother and sister; and, as husband and wife are the source, that its original tie was voluntary does not make it less close and indissoluble.

Sex is the most obvious way in which spirit and flesh meet. Hence it may be the lowest or the loftiest manifestation of human nature. The very word "love" may either have the grossest sensual meaning or be the poet's highest symbol of the noblest and holiest. As this depends on whether its well-spring is in the flesh or the spirit, no other human interest is so responsive to a religious valuation of one another.

Not only have we our Lord's supreme regard for the marriage tie, but His whole teaching rests on the idea of the family of God. And perhaps nothing shows how deep His influence has been on all who call themselves Christians as the Christian family, and this by association for duties quite as much as by association for interest, loyalty in common service being less at the mercy of change than mutual succour. Though, considering how lightly and by unlike people marriage is entered upon,

o   I

the institution is an astonishing success, natural affection needs the support of loyalty and family ties of finality. Seeing that from nothing else does the order of the State derive more strength, and that to put the tie at the mercy of the individual's good pleasure would be a material as well as a spiritual disaster, though the State may not be able to avoid consideration of special shipwreck, it is precisely the State which has to maintain public interest against private fancies.

Usually it is the advocate of spiritual interests who is accused of cant. But most of the arguments for easy divorce do not appear honest. A common one takes the chivalrous role of the defence of the woman. And apparently where divorce is easy the woman avails herself of it at least as much as the man. Nor is the reason hard to see. If her position is insecure and difficulty arises in it, she must seek her way out while she is still young and the going is good. But this itself is a vicious compulsion: and no honest thinking can doubt that a secure marriage tie, even though it may not all be of sentimental perfection, is for woman's safety and for her best and highest influence.

Though this is the most obvious example, the question of how both our honesty and our freedom stand to our natural ties and obligations and necessary undertakings is of general application: and, however we explain it, both our honesty and our freedom are much concerned in the loyalty with which we observe them and so make them not our burden but our strength and happiness. And if we regard them first for service, they will not fail to be our strength. Here above all our honesty and our freedom join in one.

CHAPTER XX

YEA AND AMEN

BESIDES the necessity of winning our freedom by rightly bearing the bondage of obligation, there is, finally, what the Apostle calls the bondage of corruption. Our honesty has to face the fact that the greatest certainty in life is death, through fear of which many are subject to bondage, and that there may be the still more overshadowing fear of disaster and failure in life while it lasts. Nor is it less certain than death itself that our powers fail, our plans are frustrated, our names are a breath, our ambitions dust, and that disappointment as well as evanescence is our inescapable destiny. Wherefore, freedom, if it is to be ours, must be won through this bondage as well as over it, by the urgency of the fleeting and the pathos of the mortal, while we are still enabled to live as if we were immortal and to do our work as though its fruits were to be everlasting.

To many this muddy vesture of decay has seemed a mere horror of pollution from which to unclothe our souls, or from which at least to shield our sensitiveness by aloofness. But this is just what honesty does not permit. Even to stand alone is so far from standing aloof, that it is then we stand most undistracted in the presence of God and are most sensitive to the needs and sorrows and evanescence of men.

It is not death only we must face alone or even times when the support of tradition, institution and kinship fail us and the heart knows its own bitterness to which our dearest friend is a stranger, but no situation is rightly met except alone with our own conscience and responsibility, not following the mass even if led by the wisest or supported by institution even the most august.

Yet to be thus alone is as far as possible from being in the void. It is rather to be most conscious of the challenge of opportunity ever on the wing, of mortal affairs as urgency to redeem the time, of the depth and tenderness mortality gives to all our human relations. To pay heed to the counsel of God, which leads to life indeed, is to redeem this life by sensitiveness to the hopes and fears around us, discernment of the signs of our ever changing and uncertain age, eagerness for what is good to know and gratitude for what is fair to behold; and is not by emptying our minds of conscious thought and considered purpose, in order to take any thought or purpose that drifts into them as the teaching and leading of the Spirit, or even to meditate on the flight of time.

The more our fellow mortals mean to us and we to them, and the fuller our lives in experience as well as service, and the more we are enriched by seeing deeper meaning and value in all, the greater and surer is the end we see beyond. For realising what is above and beyond life it is the light on life's opportunity not death's shadow over its close that is to inspire and guide: and the problem for us, especially as life goes on and the horizon narrows around us, is how to live in the power of an endless life, with courage not damped and vision not darkened, interests not diminished and tasks still done as though they and we were eternal.

What is beyond death will no doubt be the final test

of life, our works following us, the wood, hay and
stubble to be burned up, and the gold, silver and precious
stone to be shown alone in beauty, which may well leave
us sorrowfully poor. Yet, death itself is not life's greatest
test. If there be a white streak in us, the whips and scorns
of time, with long delay and failing strength, are more
likely to show it than mere fear of death. In health
many, through fear of death, are subject to bondage.
But love of life is to keep us to life's task, and there are
few not ready to depart when their call comes. It may
be rather a case of the weary who would fain sleep and
who, even in spite of their own theory, trust they sleep
to wake, than of "the strong man must go", but, in
any case, death is seldom feared at the end and often
welcomed. It is, therefore, a greater assurance that life
will not separate us from the love of God than that
death will not, for the blankness of life's futility may
sap our courage more than death itself.

In face of this no doctrine of Providence is self-
evident: and as a mere pillar of Natural Religion it is
little support, while just in loss and failure and distress
Paul finds the greatest significance of Jesus Christ's
revelation of the Father. The Apostle had been so ill
as to seem to have the sentence of death in himself, he
was still in suffering and weakness, his plans had broken
down and misrepresentation had followed, and he had to
admit a change of mind leading to a change of purpose.
But, he says, if my sole purpose is God's service, I am
not changing if I alter my plans when I find they are not
His. The Son of God Jesus Christ is never Yea and Nay,
but always Yea, meaning that if we continue in His
spirit, change itself may be consistency. Then come the

somewhat enigmatic but far-reaching words: "For how many soever be the promises of God, in Him is the Yea. Wherefore also through Him is the Amen, unto the glory of God through us." (2 Cor. i. 20.)

There used to be books of Scripture promises much studied of good people, but not of them is the Apostle thinking. It is much nearer Browning's, "What was good shall be good, with, for evil, so much good more" of all we have dreamt or thought.

But when our honesty faces life's distresses and disappointments, and searches our own heart's timidities and hesitations, is it really assured of Browning's robustious optimism? With the best and bravest of us does not life continually waver between Yea and Nay? We have inspired moments when we think diviner thoughts and would serve the glory of God in the service of man, but, apart from the assaults of worldly ambitions and oftener the arrest of faint-hearted prudence, there is the darkening of the vision with time and routine, till a life lit up in any way by the glory of God may finally pass even from desire. Hope and fear, self and self-surrender, faith and dubiety, the world and God mingle their Yea and Nay till blessed steadfastness of purpose is lost in the drifting sands of vacillation, and honesty is sorrowfully betrayed.

Only when we thus realise the danger from life's attrition and the heart's fainting, do we know the need of Jesus Christ to affirm God's glory in life, and still more, seeing how blind and deaf we are to it, to enable us to say Amen even when the glory of life is very dim to us and of the life to come very far away, with an attitude of trust and patience, which, while giving full place in our affections to their evanescence and in our labours to their futility, will enable us to carry on to the end with ever growing assurance that what we do not see God does.

Then on three points the Apostle's experience comes near our own.

First, failure in what we promise ourselves is often needed to teach us the nature of God's promises.

Second, even while we do not see we may, through Jesus Christ, both consent and co-operate.

Third, we can live in the faith that God's love in all things knows us, and cherish the hope of the blessedness of knowing it.

First, though God's promises are seen fully for us, they are never seen fully by us and seldom at all so long as we are satisfied with the success of our own plans and promises.

The Apostle had many such experiences, but it will suffice to take the last and greatest. If ever there was a worthy human purpose, it was surely his scheme of world evangelisation through the capital city to the gates of the West, with great adventure and severe labour. But it ended with writing letters in close confinement to obscure people, and martyrdom, probably in a tumult and certainly unrecorded. That thus he best served the glory of God by bringing peace and consolation to others and in being dismissed with peace and consolation to himself, upon which no activity could have improved, he could not see, and, as he accepted it, he could well say that he did not purpose according to the flesh, and, if he could be assured of the promise of God in it, he could not fail to look for it in all.

In the same hard school we also may have to be taught to look beyond our highest schemes, our most impressive works, our most applauded successes, our most admired enterprises, and learn that it is not they that are most to God's glory in man's good, and in which, therefore, is most fully God's promise. Only by frustrations and failures, it may be, can we learn the simple, sincere thoughts and the service found by willingness to be last, the promise of which is infinite and eternal.

Second, the Amen.

If we see how much wiser and better God's plan for the Apostle was than his own, he did not. But, when he recalled the surrender of the Son of God and His prayer, "Not my will but Thine be done", and realised all the blessing that came out of it, he was enabled to have the help he needed to say Amen and serve God's glory as God saw good.

How much we need such succour we know when we consider how arrogant we may be in our assumptions of wisdom, how vain of our achievements and yet how routine in our minds and how beset by negations and repressions, without inspiring vision of life's splendour or steadfast hope of its fuller consummation. Day by day we need help to say Amen, if we are to accept life's limitations in the spirit of hope and its distresses in the spirit of faith, and its conflicts in the spirit of love, with some sense of the joy set before us. And where can we find help to say it if not with One who for the joy set before Him endured the agony of the Cross and despised the shame?

Third and last, the Yea that is both direct and complete.

We are only being saved, we are to work out our salvation with fear and trembling, it may be nearer than we believed, but, from the first, we were saved by hope. In no other way do we possess it, but the difference is as the heir's who, though not having his inheritance, is sure of it. Nor does anything transform life like hope, the greatest difference between people being in what they hope for, and no life being really broken till it is without hope. Only in this sense, though a very important sense, the inheritance of the saints in light is an actual, sustaining and inspiring possession.

Yet the hope springs just from reaching out beyond our limitations. It is not a dream of Elysium, but the hope to see face to face what now we know only in broken reflexion, to know as we are known what we see now in part and guess in riddle.

This is no expectation of omniscience. The passage concludes the great lyric on love, and it is love's rule which is our concern, how nothing shall intervene in our vision of it and all be seen included in its rule. All the Apostle asks, as the consummation of his blessedness, is not a different life but a different vision, to see directly and to see wholly that all is of love, to know its rule as now we trust it knows us. Our hope thus springs from our disappointment, if our disappointment springs from the depth of our vision and unattainableness of our purpose. Not as we retire from life and become remote from men do we rise to it, but as we pursue truth till we know that our knowledge ends with what is most worth knowing, as we have fellowship with men till we know that we are separate at what is deepest in us, as we learn that what we miss of the noblest and best is just by our inability to seek it. Wherefore, the greatest that can be given us is to see all as the promise of God in love's rule in its simple directness and completeness of wisdom.

As Christ Jesus is manifest in this life, even in Him we see only in a glass darkly, yet what we see is not something different from God's rule in all, but glimpses of its deep and all-embracing dominion, enough to help us to live in the power of the hope that when the night passes and the day dawns it will be the same, yet all be changed.

One day I had been driven across the whole county of Suffolk. The spring was at the full, the variety of greens and browns infinite, the light of an unearthly perfection, under the splendour of the sky the farm houses and old world villages a changing panorama of varied beauty. Then we came to Flatford Mill, and I went in to see where Constable had first earned his bread by grinding flour for its making. I looked out of the unglazed window, as he might have done any time he lifted his head from his work, and there, framed in it, what, after all I had seen, seemed rather commonplace. But it was the scene of the Hay Wain: and Constable had done nothing to it except see it with an artist's eyes, which, however had transformed it into perfect beauty and inspired meaning.

Perhaps all we need for blessedness is for life's meaning so to unveil itself. Here in imagination we may range in the infinite, but the real infinity of meaning and value is in the common folks around, could we love and serve them better, and in the common joys and sorrows, could we respond better, and in the common tasks, were they freed from imperfections of motive and purpose. And if there be any works that follow us, will they not be the simple things in which our souls have been most open and sincerely honest and what we learned of the depths of God's wisdom and mercy, not the things of high notoriety?

The guidance of the Spirit rules out neither our foresight nor our plans, but only determines how we make them, whether as seeking God's mind or as the determined imposition of our own, whether we think we succeed with them only as we drive them through or whether we are open to the belief that their purpose is to lead us to a point where we may see a better way, or, if they are frustrated, to believe if we do not see, that it is for a higher end.

There has been so much you confidently, possibly justly, thought the promises of God, the things you saw in an inspired moment and consecrated yourselves to follow when the Spirit was on you. They came to you as good children of God speaking of diviner thoughts and higher purposes and the glory of God in nobler service. Nothing you can owe to Jesus Christ can be greater than the power to cherish them in honest loyalty to the highest given you to see and the noblest to follow till you know that the inheritance of the saints in light is only the open and complete vision of what you have sought in weakness and perplexity and disappointment. Doubtless that will be our full salvation, but we best seek God's next stage for us as in honesty we commit ourselves to the liberty wherewith Christ has set us free in respect of the discipline and duty of the present hour.

INDEX

CAMBRIDGE: PRINTED BY W. LEWIS M.A., AT THE UNIVERSITY PRESS